DRUGS POLICY IN DEVELOPING COUNTRIES

DRUGS POLICY IN DEVELOPING COUNTRIES

Najmi Kanji, Anita Hardon, Jan Willem Harnmeijer,
Masuma Mamdani and Gill Walt

Zed Books Ltd

London and New Jersey

Drugs Policy in Developing Countries was first published by
Zed Books Ltd, 57 Caledonian Road, London N1 9BU, UK, and
165 First Avenue, Atlantic Highlands, New Jersey 07716, USA,
in 1992.

Copyright © Najmi Kanji, Anita Hardon, Jan Willem Harnmeijer,
Masuma Mamdani, Gill Walt, 1992.

Cover designed by Andrew Corbett.
Laserset by Selro Publishing Services, Oxford.
Printed and bound in the United Kingdom
by Biddles Ltd, Guildford and King's Lynn.

A catalogue record for this book is
available from the British Library.

US CIP is available from
the Library of Congress.

ISBN 1 85649 059 9 Hb
ISBN 1 85649 060 2 Pb

**Published with the support of the Danish
International Development Agency (DANIDA).**

Contents

Tables and Figures   vi
Contributors   vii
Foreword and Acknowledgements   ix
Acronyms and Abbreviations   xi

1   Early Initiatives in Essential Drugs Policy
      Masuma Mamdani   1

      Drugs and Health in Developing Countries   1
      The Domination by the Transnational Drugs Industries   3
      Chaos Turns to Tragedy   5
      Drugging the Americas   7
      The Response of the Third World   8
      The Search for a Way Forward   11
      The World Health Organization   12
      Cooperation with other UN Agencies   14
      A Coordinated UN Response   16
      The Industry's Response   17
      Conclusion   19

2   Formulating an Essential Drugs Policy: WHO's Role
      Gill Walt and Jan Willem Harnmeijer   24

      WHO's Structure and Policy Processes   24
      Getting Essential Drugs on to the Policy Agenda   26
      The Period of Policy Exploration 1977-1981   27
      Setting the Priorities: 1981-1983   28
      Advocacy and Action: 1983-1988   33
      Policy Drift: 1988-1990   42

3   **Consumers versus Producers:**
     Power Play Behind the Scenes
     Anita Hardon   48

     Introduction   48
     The Early Years of DAP   49
     Calling for a Code on Pharmaceutical Marketing   50
     Heightened Politicization: The Industry on the Defensive   52
     The Nairobi Conference: 1985   55
     The Revised Drugs Strategy   58
     More Emphasis on National-level Implementation: 1986-90   60
     In Conclusion   62

4   **Action at Country Level:**
     The International and National Influences
     Najmi Kanji   65

     Components of a Rational Drugs Policy   65
     International Drug Companies   69
     The World Health Organization   74
     Donors   76
     UNICEF   78
     The National Connection   79

5   **What Has Been Achieved and Where Are We Now?**
     Najmi Kanji and Anita Hardon   91

     Essential Drugs Lists   91
     Essential Drugs Programmes   93
     The Availability of Essential Drugs   96
     The Rational Use of Drugs   98
     Assessing Rational Drugs Use   98
     Self-medication: A Constraint to the Success of EDPs   100
     The Irrationality of Diarrhoea Treatment   101
     Antibiotic Misuse: Far-reaching Consequences   102
     Rationality in a Socio-cultural Perspective   102
     Have 15 Years of Essential Drugs Achieved Anything?   103

6   New Horizons in the 1990s
Anita Hardon and Najmi Kanji   110

The Leadership Role of WHO Diminishes   110
Pharmaceutical Cost Recovery and Structural Adjustment   113
The Rational Use of Drugs: Focus for the 1990s   115
AIDS and Increasing Demands for Drugs   117
The Rational Use of Contraceptives: Free Choice?   118
Rationalizing the Private Sector: The Industry's Role   119
In Conclusion   123

Appendix   128
Index   133

Tables and Figures

Tables

2.1   DAP: Financial Resources (1980-9) for Global and
          Interregional Activities   34
2.2   Staffing Levels of DAP, Geneva   35
5.1   The Drugs Market from 13 Country Case Studies   92
5.2   Distribution of Essential Drugs to Primary Level Services   97

Figures

5.1   Countries with Essential Drugs Lists, 1983-9   92
5.2   Countries with Operational Essential Drugs
          Programmes, 1983 and 1989   93

Contributors

Najmi Kanji

Before becoming a research fellow in the Health Policy Unit at the London School of Hygiene and Tropical Medicine, Najmi Kanji spent seven years in Mozambique working on issues related to drugs and health policy. He is currently developing collaborative research in Tanzania, Angola and Brazil to assess the quality of their primary level health services. He is also working on issues related to structural adjustment programmes and their effects on health.

Anita Hardon

Anita Hardon (Ph.D.) is a medical biologist in the Medical Anthropology Unit of the University of Amsterdam. Having undertaken research into the use and distribution of pharmaceuticals in the Philippines between 1985 and 1988, she is presently involved in projects concerned with pharmaceutical cost recovery and the use of contraceptives and injections. She is the research coordinator of the Amsterdam-based Women's Health Action Foundation's project on women and pharmaceuticals.

Jan Willem Harnmeijer

For many years since 1975 Jan Willem Harnmeijer worked as a medical doctor in Tanzania, Kenya, Botswana, the Sudan and Zambia to promote the essential drugs activities of various comprehensive primary health care (PHC) programmes. Though his experience is in PHC in general, he is particularly interested in the planning, managing and financing of PHC programmes. He is currently working in the PHC unit at the Royal Tropical Institute in Amsterdam. He holds an MPH and an M.Sc. in health planning and finance.

Masuma Mamdani

Born in Uganda, Masuma Mamdani was educated at Wellesley College and the University of California and Los Angeles (UCLA) where she took her MPH. After working for five years in Tanzania, she came to the London School of Hygiene and Tropical Medicine, where she is now an epidemiologist and Research Fellow specializing in drugs policy, maternal health and AIDS. Her articles have appeared in various learned journals, including *Health Policy and Planning, Family Planning Studies* and the *East African Medical Journal.*

Gill Walt

Gill Walt is senior lecturer in health policy and head of the Health Policy Unit at the London School of Hygiene and Tropical Medicine. Her main interests are in public policy and much of her research has been on the shift in health policy towards primary health care. This has included both a concern with policy processes (such as the influence of international organizations like the World Health Organization on national health policy) and on policy content (such as essential drugs, the problems of supervizing traditional birth attendants or employing community health workers). She has worked in Mozambique for three years and for shorter periods in several countries in southern Africa, as well as in Sri Lanka and Brazil. Her most recent book is *Community Health Workers in National Programmes: Just Another Pair of Hands?* (Open University Press, 1990).

Foreword and Acknowledgements

Despite the potential benefits of drugs, in many developing countries the annual per capita expenditure on them remains below US$1 and it is estimated that 1,300-2,500 million people have little or no regular access to essential drugs. This is despite the fact that, for many developing countries, drugs expenditure can amount to 20-30 per cent of their annual health budgets. On the other hand, total world drugs consumption in 1990 was about US$200,000 million, of which around 50 per cent was controlled by the top 25 European and US multinationals. Though generically produced essential drugs are available at prices most developing countries can afford, few policies have been developed to promote essential drugs and control the excesses of business interests. Many influences have been brought to bear on countries attempting to rationalize their drugs systems, ranging from strikes by doctors and pharmacists to the threatened cutting off of aid. The issue of essential drugs thus overflows from the health sector to touch the very core of economic and political ideologies and it remains an important factor in development.

The last few years have seen a major move towards the commoditization of health in the developed world and the transfer of this ideology to the developing world. Within this free market concept of health, rationalizing drugs policies and controlling multinational companies is seen as interference by the state. It is important to raise the issues involved in promoting rational drugs policies, especially now that Eastern Europe and South Africa are planning their new health systems.

In 1989, at the request of various donor and recipient governments, the London School of Hygiene and Tropical Medicine (LSHTM) and the Royal Tropical Institute in Amsterdam (KIT) carried out a year long evaluation of WHO's Action Programme on Essential Drugs. The evaluation included not only a policy review and an assessment of the programme in WHO in Geneva, but also 13 country studies and reports on WHO's five regional offices. In addition, interviews were carried out with members of the pharmaceutical industry and consumer organizations. By its very nature, the final report could not include all of the information collected during the year. This book takes that material as its starting point and looks at the evolution of rational drugs policies in developing countries, problems and constraints in their implementation and likely future scenarios.

The book has four specific objectives. These are to document the essential drugs 'story' at the international and national levels; to analyse and illustrate the complexity of the policy process with regard to essential drugs in order to outline crucial steps in policy formulation; to assist policy makers and interested parties to understand the issues involved in policy development so that they are better able to consider options available for action; and to draw out the major issues likely to influence future policies for essential drugs.

This book will be of interest to policy makers and academics in both developing and developed countries, to students and teachers on health courses or postgraduate courses concerned with health issues, and to managers and decision makers involved in health and essential drugs programmes in NGOs, international agencies and government institutions, particularly Ministries of Health. We also hope that various international agencies or other organizations will find the book useful in understanding some of the problems involved in policy definition and implementation and thus provide lessons for the future.

Finally, we wish to acknowledge the generous financial support given by the Danish International Development Agency (DANIDA) for the research and writing of this book. We particularly wish to thank Mr Neils Dabelstein of DANIDA's Evaluation Unit and colleagues in the APED evaluation team, Wilbert Bannenberg, Susan Rifkin and Peter Streefland. Many others, too numerous to mention by name, gave generously of their time, knowledge and information, as consultants to the evaluation team both at the international and national level and as hosts and interviewers in many countries. WHO personnel, both within and outside the Drugs Action Programme, were unfailingly courteous and helpful, as were the numerous NGOs and donors. Without the contribution of all these people, this book would not have been possible.

The Editors

Acronyms and Abbreviations

ACDIMA	Arab Company for Drug Industries and Medical Appliances
ADM	kaolin/pectin anti-diarrhoeal medicine
AFRO	Africa Regional Office (of WHO)
ALIFABOL	Drug producers' association in Bolivia
APEC	Action Programme for Economic Cooperation
APED	Action Programme on Essential Drugs
ASEAN	Association of Southeast Asian Nations
ASOFAR	Association of importers in Bolivia
CMO	Chief Medical Officer
COPPTECS	Cooperative Pharmaceutical Production and Technology Centres
DANIDA	Danish International Development Agency
DAP	Drugs Action Programme
DDS	drugs and dietary supplement kits
DIAC	Drug Information and Action Centre (Thailand)
DMP	Division of Drug Management and Policies
DPM	Drug Policies and Management unit within WHO
EB	Executive Board
EDLs	Essential Drugs Lists
EDLIZ	Essential Drugs List of Zimbabwe
EDP	Essential Drugs Programme
EMRO	Eastern Mediterranean Regional Office
EURO	European Regional Office (of WHO)
FARMAC	Mozambican state pharmaceutical company
HAI	Health Action International
HAIN	Health Action Information Network (Philippines)
IBFAN	International Baby Food Action Network
ICIFI	International Council of Infant Food Industries
IFPMA	International Federation of Pharmaceutical Manufacturers Associations
ILO	International Labour Office
IMI	Institute for Medical Informatics
INASME	Central drugs' importing agency in Bolivia
INFACT	Infant Formula Action Coalition
INRUD	International Network for the Rational Use of Drugs
IOCU	International Organization of Consumer Unions
IOMS	International Organization Monitoring Services
JCHP	Joint Committee on Health Policy

KIT	Koninklijk Instituut voor de Tropen
LSHTM	London School of Hygiene and Tropical Medicine
MEDIMOC	Mozambican state drugs importing company
MLAM	Medical Lobby for Appropriate Marketing
MOH	Ministry of Health
MSH	Management Sciences for Health
MTI	Ministry of Trade and Industry
NAPCO	Tanzanian parastatal importing company
NGOs	Non-governmental organizations
NHS	National Health Service
ORT	oral rehydration therapy
OTC	over the counter
PAHO	Pan American Health Organization (of WHO)
PDRY	People's Democratic Republic of Yemen
PEDLIZ	Proposed Essential Drugs List of Zimbabwe
PHA	Pharmaceuticals unit within WHO
PHC	Primary Health Care
PMA	Pharmaceutical Manufacturers Association (US)
PMC	Programme Management Committee
PS	Principal Secretary
RAD-AR	Risk Assessment of Drugs: Analysis and Response
SEARO	South-East Asia Regional Office
SGS	Société Général de Surveillance
SIDA	Swedish International Development Agency
SMON	sub-acute myelo-optic neuropathy
SPC	State Pharmaceutical Corporation (Sri Lanka)
TCDC	Technical Cooperation among the Developing Countries
TNCs	transnational corporations
UN	United Nations
UNCTAD	United Nations Conference on Trade and Development
UNCTC	United Nations Centre on Transnational Corporations
UNDP	United Nations Development Programme
UNESC	United Nations Economic and Social Council
UNESCO	United Nations Educational, Cultural and Scientific Organization
UNFPA	United Nations Family Planning Association
UNICEF	United Nations Children's Fund
UNIDO	United Nations Industrial Development Organization
UNIPAC	UNICEF Packing and Assembly Centre
USAID	United States Agency for International Development
VHAI	Voluntary Health Action International
WEMOS	The Working Group on Medical Development Aid
WHA	World Health Assembly
WHO	World Health Organization
WPRO	Western Pacific Regional Office (of WHO)
YAR	Yemen Arab Republic
ZEDAP	Zimbabwean Essential Drugs Programme

1

Early Initiatives in Essential Drugs Policy

Masuma Mamdani

Thirty years ago modern health technology had just awakened and was full of promise. Since then, its expansion has surpassed all dreams, only to become a nightmare. For it has become over sophisticated and over costly. It is dictating our health policies unwisely; and what is useful is being applied to too few. Based on these technologies, a huge medical industry has grown up with powerful vested interests of its own. Like the sorcerer's apprentice, we have lost control, social control, over health technology. The slave of our imagination has become the master of our creativity. We must now learn to control it again and use it wisely, in the struggle for health freedom. This struggle is important for all countries; for developing countries it is crucial.

These words from Dr Halfden Mahler's report to the 31st World Health Assembly (WHA) in 1978 are particularly appropriate when they are applied to pharmaceutical technology and the drugs industry. This chapter, which is basically an attempt to examine the pharmaceutical situation in the developing world up to the mid-1970s, discusses three core issues. These are domination by the transnational drugs companies, the adverse effects of certain drugs and the unethical marketing practices which were brought to the public's attention during the 1970s and alerted health policy-makers at both the international and national level to the need for rationalization in this important area of health care. The chapter then describes the early attempts of some developing countries to rationalize their drugs supply systems and the initiatives of United Nations (UN) organizations to support and promote these countries in their efforts. But before going on to look at the domination of the drugs companies, we need to understand some of the problems associated with pharmaceuticals in the less developed world.

Drugs and Health in Developing Countries

In 1975, a World Bank policy paper concluded that the major causes of poor health in developing countries were malnutrition, inadequate sanitary conditions and poor housing (World Bank, 1975). Although lasting improvement

1

in people's health is dependent on long-range improvements in their economic, political and social environments, disease and disability fostered by these factors can often be cured or controlled by the appropriate use of drugs. In addition, the availability and effectiveness of drugs are key factors in generating and maintaining public interest and participation in health related activities.

Despite their potentially beneficial health impact, the annual per capita expenditure for drugs remains below US$1 in many developing countries. The World Health Organization (WHO) estimated that in 1985 between 1,300 and 2,500 million people in the developing world had little or no regular access to essential drugs (WHO, 1988). None the less, a government's drugs bill may account for up to 40 per cent of its overall annual health budget, making the efficient management of drugs expenditure a vital consideration for health planners (WHO, 1977).

The growing market for pharmaceuticals in the third world has to be seen within the context of the political and economic transformation of those countries during the colonial period which, for some, ended only in the 1950s and 1960s. Colonization resulted in the penetration of the cultures and social institutions of the ruling country. In most developing countries the outcome of this was a curative system for the urban minority with only minimal resources provided for rural health care. The provision of government services for the indigenous population was primarily motivated by a concern to protect the white colonials from infectious diseases and potential epidemics and to maintain a relatively healthy and, thus, productive 'native' labour force. Access to medical services in the rural areas was limited and selective (Basch, 1990: 3-27, 74-99).

The newly independent developing countries became an important and a rapidly expanding market for the transnational drugs companies. It was to their advantage that the health services remained oriented towards a curative approach. Virtually all their advertising effort was and is aimed at the promotion of products used for curative medicine. By the 1970s many developing countries were spending a large proportion of their public health budget on drugs. In 1976 Thailand spent 30.4 per cent of its government health budget on drugs. For Bangladesh the proportion was 63.7 per cent (1976) (UNESC, 1981: 4). Yet the majority of people living in rural areas and urban slums, the principal victims of endemic and epidemic diseases, had no or only marginal access to treatment with 'modern' drugs. This scarcity was partly because, within the limited available resources, health had to compete alongside a number of equally deserving needs (for example, education and agriculture). Compared to the developed countries, most developing nations spend a very small percentage of their gross national product on health (UNESC, 1981). At the same time drugs were being imported at relatively high prices, often out of proportion to their effectiveness and the purchasing power of the poor. Furthermore, the retail prices paid by patients and even Ministries of Health were often subjected to substantial mark-ups by local distributors and businessmen. In Bangladesh, for example, these accounted for up to two thirds of the retail price (Bangladesh MOH, 1977).

The character of the inherited colonial health system did not change dramatically following independence. Although equitable distribution of health services and an emphasis on the previously neglected rural areas were specified as a part of the national socio-economic development policy, the large urban hospitals tended to absorb a major fraction of the available resources, both financial and human. For example, 79 per cent of Tanzania's 1977 drugs budget was allocated to hospitals, 14 per cent to dispensaries and only 7 per cent to health centres (Yudkin, 1980); and, in Bangladesh, 75 per cent of the money spent on curative health services was channelled through health facilities in the towns where only 8 per cent of the population lived (Melrose, 1982). This picture was reflected even in those countries that had gained independence many years before. Resource allocation to rural development remained skewed throughout the third world: 'financial allocations, determined politically, did not match the ambitions created' (Lunde et al., 1989).

Paradoxically, however, the private sector market in pharmaceuticals was flooded with thousands of inappropriate preparations under a bewildering choice of brand names, all at a prohibitive cost for a major fraction of the population. In 1957 Egypt had a total of 80,000 brand names on the market (Lauridsen, 1984: 4-6); Brazil and Argentina had around 24,000 and 17,000 respectively (1970s) (Mamdani and Walker, 1985: 12). The situation was not very different in some of the Western European countries, especially in the drugs producing nations: 36,000 brand names in Switzerland (Muller, 1982); and about 15,000 each in the Federal Republic of Germany and in the United Kingdom (Dukes, 1985: 12).

Overall, the drugs picture that emerged in the 1970s was of an excessive waste of resources in the third world. The proliferation of drugs, in the absence of the necessary infrastructure and trained personnel for the efficient and safe distribution of medicines, has led to the evolution of a chaotic and indiscriminate system of drugs distribution and use. It was a situation aggravated by the lack of accurate and objective drugs information and inadequate or non-existent regulatory controls in most developing countries. Food supplements and tonics of dubious nutritional and pharmacological value often made up a high proportion of the total drugs bill. Irrational, expensive and dangerous combinations of drugs were common and a serious mismatch existed between drugs needed to treat real health needs and those that were available.

The Domination by the Transnational Drugs Industries

The pharmaceutical industry in developing countries represented a formidable challenge to policy-makers and continues to present a complex set of problems. To begin with, the structure of the industry is dominated by large transnational corporations (TNCs). They are a formidable force. Fifteen of these monoliths each had world sales of US$1,000-2,400 million in 1980, which is more than the gross national product of many third world countries (Medawar, 1985). Over the past four decades world pharmaceutical sales have become increasingly concentrated in the hands of a small number of companies, about 25, which accounted for about 60 per cent of total production (UNCTC, 1979). Almost 70 per cent of world production of pharmaceutical products took place in only five developed market economy countries: Britain, France, Switzerland, West Germany and the USA (UNIDO, 1980).

Developing countries, with three-quarters of the world's population, produced less than 10 per cent of the world's drugs and accounted for less than a quarter of the annual global expenditure on drugs, which was estimated to be US$100,000 million in early 1984 (WHO, 1984). A closer look reveals that over two-thirds of that production comes from relatively few countries (India, Cuba, Egypt, Argentina, Brazil and Mexico) which meet most local needs in finished products, ranging from 83 per cent of local consumption in Egypt to 97 per cent in Mexico. Most other developing countries continue to depend on imports for a majority of their drugs needs. New drugs were mainly produced and marketed for the rich world, with its greater purchasing power and per capita expenditure in the late 1970s noted to be 20 times higher than that of developing countries (Mamdani and Walker, 1985).

TNCs often act with a high degree of autonomy. Their strategies and behaviour, however, varies from one country to another. Marked international differences exist in prices of the same drugs, indicating that the companies price their drugs according to 'what a particular national market will bear and the degree of control exercised by local authorities over cost' (UNCTAD, 1977). For example, as UNESC (1981: 4) shows:

> In Argentina, the prices of drugs in eight submarkets were found to be 143 to 3,700 [sic] per cent higher than the minimum prices at which the same products were imported by the same country.... In Mexico's steroid hormone sector, progesterone was imported by one firm in 1972 at US$2,490 per kilogram and exported by another firm from Mexico in the same year for $110 per kilo. Extradiol was exported from Mexico by Syntex for $880 a kilogram, and imported into the country by another foreign subsidiary in the same year for $80,000 a kilo. In Brazil, a parliamentary inquiry found several instances of overpricing ranging from 500 to 1,000 per cent.

Another means by which TNCs maximize their profits from developing countries is to over value the raw materials their subsidiaries import from the parent firm and to under value the products they export back to it. Thus, their insistence on imposing restrictive conditions when they establish their subsidiaries and affiliates, as a prerequisite for their cooperation in the development of national industries, further buttresses their power. An examination of the overall investment pattern of TNCs in South American subsidiaries between 1957 and 1965 (Fajnzylber, 1971: 17) showed that 83 per cent of the gross investment came from sources within the host country (local savings or reinvested earnings of the subsidiary) and that, between 1960 and 1968, the very same TNCs repatriated 79 per cent of the net profits. A report by the Indian Institute of Public Administration (George, 1990: 99) shows that, in 1976 alone, the 189 Indian TNC affiliates which made up the sample not only earned no foreign exchange but actually cost the country a minimum of US$25 million.

It is frequently claimed that the presence of TNCs operating in developing countries actively assists 'development' by a steady transfer of technology. Indeed, in the 1970s many developing countries argued this point and some UN agencies tried to assist in the transfer of pharmaceutical technology. This turned out to be much more difficult than originally envisaged, partly because the structure and power of TNCs depends on their retention of total control over such technology. As it turned out, there has been virtually no transfer of relevant technology by these companies to the countries of the developing world. In fact, by using the power that control over technology brings, they have eliminated many potential competitors and prevented indigenous pharmaceutical industries from developing to meet the real needs of the people of the third world.

Chaos Turns to Tragedy

Between 1956 and 1970 an epidemic swept through Japan, leaving more than 10,000 people suffering from paralysis and partial or total loss of sight (Chetley and Gilbert, 1986). The disease was called SMON (sub-acute myelo-optic neuropathy), a serious nervous system damage caused by regular intake of clioquinol, once seen as a 'promising anti-amoebic drug'. Despite the hazards, Ciba-Geigy, the most important manufacturer of the drug, did not remove its clioquinol products from the world market until March 1985. It has been argued that Ciba-Geigy refused to concede that the drug was dangerous, partly because clioquinol had been a 'profitable drug for decades' and partly because 'withdrawal of the drug would have weakened its legal position' (Chetley and Gilbert, 1986: 1).

Most Western countries only became concerned about the safety of drugs around 30 years ago. Improved standards for new medicines in Britain (Collier, 1985) can be attributed to the consumption of a drug with particularly hazardous adverse effects, thalidomide. Thalidomide was first marketed in November 1956 for use in a wide range of conditions, including influenza, functional disorders of the stomach and gall bladder, mild depression and menstrual tension. Widely promoted as a safe and effective drug to be used during pregnancy, it resulted in the birth of some 6,000 severely deformed babies (Chetley and Gilbert, 1986).

Huge public concern in Britain over the thalidomide disaster in 1961 focused on the compounding hazards of medication. This stimulated the establishment of a national drugs regulatory agency called the Committee on Safety of Medicines (formerly the Dunlop Committee), the Medicines Act (1968) and a multitude of codes of practice for advertising issued by bodies such as the Institute of British Advertisers and the Advertising Standards Authority (Collier, 1985). In Norway, where drugs safety legislation was introduced as long ago as 1928, there are only about 1,000 brands of medicines available for prescribing (Medawar, 1984). Apart from drugs safety and efficacy considerations, special features in Norwegian legislation have been 'the clause of need' (medical justification) and 'the five-years rule' of reconsideration. The first clause makes it possible to reject new products of appropriate quality if medical needs are covered qualitatively and quantitatively by products already on the market. The second clause implies that the necessity for every drug is formally reconsidered by the drugs registration authorities at five-year intervals (Lunde, 1982).

Medicines produced in Western countries for export did not always meet the same high standards of safety and efficacy as those intended for sale in the country of manufacture. Drugs exports in Switzerland and Britain, for example, have been specifically exempted from such regulatory controls (Kay, 1976). Thus, some drugs which had been superseded by more effective pharmaceuticals in many Western industrialized countries, continued to be available in the third world. Some of these had been withdrawn from the market in industrialized countries because they were either harmful or ineffective; others had never been marketed in industrialized countries.

Most developing countries imported almost all their drugs and lacked the necessary infrastructure with which to regulate their quality. Thus, actions of this nature taken in industrialized countries rarely got conveyed to other countries. Furthermore, the information the drugs companies supplied to regulatory authorities and prescribers to ensure the safe and proper use of their products was not always reliable. Far from being scrupulously consistent and based on scientific principles, it differed markedly from country to country (Silverman, 1976).

Once a drug is on the market it is very difficult to restrict its usage, even if hazards are identified. In Western countries, for example, it took at least ten years to restrict the use of chloramphenicol, a potent, potentially toxic antibiotic, the dangers of which had already been widely publicized. Though mainly prescribed for 'certain life-threatening infections which could not be adequately treated with a safer drug', in developing countries it continued to be prescribed for trivial indications, which resulted in chloramphenicol resistant typhoid fever in several parts of the world (Herxheimer, 1984). In Mexico, in 1972, its misuse caused typhoid fever death rates similar to those of the pre-antibiotic era (WHO, 1977a). Lack of data on adverse drugs reactions in developing countries often meant that they were wished away. For example, in 1975 an editorial in an Asian medical journal claimed that 'chloramphenicol does not produce the same hazards or complications as in European societies' (Medawar, 1984: 34).

By the mid-1970s the seriousness of the situation was gaining international attention. The new director-general of WHO, Dr Halfden Mahler, said in his report to the World Health Assembly (WHA) (WHO, 1975):

Drugs not authorized for sale in the country of origin, or withdrawn from the market for reasons of safety or lack of efficacy, are sometimes exported and marketed in developing countries. Other drugs are promoted and advertised in those countries for indications that are not approved by the regulatory agencies of the country of origin. Products not meeting the quality requirements of the exporting country, including products beyond their expiry date, may be exported to developing countries that are not in a position to carry out quality control measures. While these practices may conform to legal requirements, they are unethical and detrimental to health.

Drugging the Americas

In the second half of the 1970s a number of publications, of which the most salient was *The Drugging of the Americas* (Silverman, 1976), drew attention to the unethical marketing practices of the multinational drugs industry. Methods of promotion were found to be more ruthless in the third world, where controlling legislation was generally more lax and difficult to implement. Advertising was used to manipulate and create life styles. Its function was to stimulate brand consciousness to increase sales. Pharmaceutical industries created a demand for the most profitable of their patented drugs. Usually, such demands bore a limited relation to actual needs. The industry's first and very necessary priority was to make a profit. As one industry spokesman (Teeling-Smith, 1977) commented, 'I would just be talking rubbish if I were to say that the multinational companies were operating in the less developed countries primarily for the welfare of those countries.... They are not bishops, they are businessmen.'

Not only was the industry selling its own branded drugs at an enormous profit, but it was also reinforcing the belief that there is 'a pill for every ill'. In pursuit of a frequently illusory therapy, poor people were often spending large parts of their incomes on inessential and hazardous drugs. In most instances drugs representatives were the only source of information to doctors in remote areas. Besides, it was common practice for doctors not only to examine and prescribe for their patients, but also to sell the drugs to the patients. In India doctors account for the sale of a large volume of drugs and, not surprisingly, the drugs representatives visit them frequently (Anonymous, 1970). Orders are placed directly with sales representatives for those drugs that offer significant profit margins, rather than for those that may best meet the patients' needs. Some doctors earn more from the sale of drugs than from consultation fees.

Even if health professionals had no direct monetary incentive to promote, misuse and massively over prescribe drugs, limited time for large numbers of patients, the 'pill for every ill' ethos and the attainment of credibility through prescribing drugs that patients really want, has led to an over use of drugs. The indiscriminate use of antibiotics led to widespread outbreaks of diseases caused by antibiotic-resistant bacteria (Melrose, 1982):

In 1969 an epidemic of Shiga dysentery killed 12,500 people in Guatemala and 2,000 more in El Salvador. The disease was resistant to chloramphenicol, tetracycline, streptomycin and sulphonamide drugs. Three years later there was an outbreak of typhoid affecting over 6,000 people in Mexico. As with the strain of typhoid reported in India that year, the drug of choice, chloramphenicol, proved useless.

The promotional activities of drugs companies strongly influenced the purchase and prescribing of drugs in all countries; the lack of government policies exacerbated the situation. When no guidelines existed for standards of health care, or for the role of doctors, the field was open to manipulation for profit.

The Response of the Third World

In the early 1960s and 1970s governments of several third world countries, such as Costa Rica, Cuba, Egypt, India, Mexico, Mozambique, Pakistan, Peru and Sri Lanka, attempted to rationalize their purchase of medicines. The measures they took ranged from stepping-up local production of drugs to bulk purchasing a limited number of essential drugs in their generic form. Some were more successful than others.

Cuba, for example, has made continuous efforts over the last 25 years or so to overcome its external drugs dependence which, in 1958, amounted to 70-80 per cent of all drugs supplies, mainly in the finished form (Capo, 1983). By 1980, 81 per cent of the country's total requirements were satisfied by national production. Two distinctive features were instrumental in Cuba's success: a strong national quality control infrastructure and a good centralized procurement system, with efficient market intelligence to provide the necessary information with which to obtain quality drugs on optimum terms.

In Egypt, most of the pharmaceutical industry was nationalized in the early 1960s and, as such, did not have to fight a protracted battle against the TNCs in the market. Its dealings with the TNCs were built on a strong position based on protectionism (UNESC, 1981: 4). Nasser's 1952 revolution of self-reliance and social justice was instrumental in the implementation of a radical drugs policy in 1957, which enabled the national industry to consolidate its dwindling and unprotected market share (Galal, 1983). Its success was remarkable. By 1961 the government had achieved full control of around 90 per cent of national production and, by 1962, under the policy guidance of the Ministry of Health, the nationalization of the drugs industry had been implemented with a state monopoly on imports, production, distribution and planning. Drugs consumption between 1952 and 1961 increased by 310 per cent (from E£4.8 million to E£14.9 million) and by 488 per cent (to E£72.8 million) from 1961 to 1974, with local production covering about 85 per cent in 1974, despite fighting a major war in 1972.

As 1975 approached Egypt's political and economic orientation began to change. It sought accommodation instead of confrontation. 'Subdued alignment' replaced non-alignment. The consumer economy became more important than self-reliance. One result of this was that the share of the national industry slowly declined (Galal, 1983: 237).

The potential for price rivalry among pharmaceutical companies was greatest in the generic drugs market, which had been expanding rapidly since the 1960s in both developed and developing countries (UNCTC, 1979). This was mainly due to the expiration of patents on many drugs, the entry of new firms into the production of generic products and the desire of many countries to reduce the costs of pharmaceuticals. The price of a leading brand was often five times higher than the price of unbranded (generic) versions of the identical drug in both developing and developed countries (Medawar, 1984).

While a policy of introducing generic prescriptions in the pharmaceutical market achieved significant results in Cuba, Costa Rica and Sri Lanka, it failed in Pakistan (UNCTAD, 1980; UNCTAD, 1982; Lall and Bibile, 1978). The reasons given for this failure were said to be that neither doctors nor the public were informed of the benefits, that there was concerted opposition from the TNCs and that a lack of quality control checks had led to a flood of sub-standard drugs onto the market and, consequently, in 1977, to a reversal of Pakistan's policy four years after it had been introduced (Agarwal, 1978).

Mozambique tackled the structure of the pharmaceutical market by nationalizing its health service a month after independence in 1975. The Frelimo government's social policy on health was greatly influenced by the experiences of the independence movement in the liberated zones during the war. The cornerstones of the policy were strict drugs registration and an effective national formulary which, by 1980, had reduced therapeutic items in different dosage forms and strengths from 13,000 to 343. In 1977 this control was further reinforced with the establishment of MEDIMOC, a state drugs importing company. As a result of these measures, Mozambique managed to quadruple the quantity of pharmaceuticals imported without a significant increase in foreign exchange spending. Unfortunately, the outbreak of war in the early 1980s resulted in a deteriorating economic situation which, in turn, undermined the national health strategy. Free drugs packages provided by international agencies further exacerbated this situation (Mamdani and Walker, 1985).

Costa Rica has, however, been more successful. In importing drugs it has achieved substantial savings for the public sector by establishing centralized procurement in bulk form through a public tender system and adhering to a list of essential drugs (UNESC, 1981: 4). The resultant savings enabled the Costa Rican government to increase its funding to meet local drugs needs (Mamdani and Walker, 1985). Brazil's central procurement agency, *Central de Medicamentos*, is also estimated to have saved about 60 per cent by purchasing a restricted number of generic drugs with functional packaging (UNCTC, 1984). Bulk purchasing in Egypt helped keep the prices of pharmaceuticals constant for 18 years and, at the same time, created a favourable climate for the development of the country's strong local industry (SCRIP, 1981).

Sri Lanka, faced with a chronic foreign exchange problem and a 40-50 per cent increase in drugs prices, found that the 1970 allocation of foreign exchange could buy only half the drugs purchased by the 1965 allocation (Wickremasinghe and Bibile, 1971: 757). In 1972 Sri Lanka extended the sale and use of generic names, already enforced in the public health services in 1959, to the private sector and set up a State Pharmaceutical Corporation (SPC) to centralize drugs imports, which had now been reduced to 600 (Lall, 1979). In 1973 the government announced its new '34 Drug Programme', under which the chemical intermediates needed for local formulation of the 34 basic drugs best considered to meet the health needs of the country were to be centrally procured by the SPC. While 'some problems were encountered with the quality of a few drugs, and these were seized upon and publicized by opponents of the reform, there is little doubt that the overall benefits far exceeded its (probably inherent) risks even in the early stages' (Lall, 1979: 236). The savings achieved were considerable, about 40 per cent in the first six months.

Sri Lanka's experience also demonstrated that a process of re-education, coupled with careful control over the quality of generic drugs, can to some extent succeed in rationalizing prescribing practices. An essential drugs list facilitated the provision of more accurate information on the use of drugs than was normally provided by market mechanisms (UNCTAD, 1977). In Mozambique, a rigid government bulk purchasing policy, linked to an effective national formulary, led to the virtual disappearance of drugs representatives and of advertising without direct intervention (Marzagao and Segall, 1983). Likewise, the Costa Rican government had long introduced strict controls over the promotion of both prescription only and over the counter medicines (UNCTC, 1979; UNESC, 1981: 4).

In Sri Lanka, rationalizing imports of pharmaceutical chemicals for local formulation proved to be much more difficult than for finished drugs. The country faced strong opposition from the five multinationals manufacturing drugs on the island. One US company, Pfizer, stalled negotiations over local production plans for four years. It even refused an urgent appeal from the SPC to make tetracycline capsules for the cholera epidemic of 1974. The main issue was that the raw materials were to be supplied by Hoechst via the SPC and 'Pfizer had traditionally paid its parent company $99 per kilogram while Hoechst was offering to supply it for just $20' (Muller, 1982: 22). This dissatisfaction was further expressed by the US Pharmaceutical Manufacturers Association (PMA), whose president 'wrote personally to the Sri Lankan Prime Minister outlining his numerous objections to the scheme which, he said, "calls in question the Government's position with respect to all foreign investment in Sri Lanka"'(Muller, 1982: 22). Attempts to nationalize Pfizer, purely out of frustration on the part of the Sri Lankan government, resulted in a threat from the US ambassador, who 'indicated that the supply of food aid from his country would be put in serious jeopardy by such an action' (Muller, 1982: 22).

While the achievements of reform in Sri Lanka were impressive, 'resistance from multinational affiliates, drugs importers and the medical profession continued and the change of government in 1977 led to some emasculation of the activities of the SPC' (Lall, 1979: 236). Sri Lanka continues to be dependent upon imports for the bulk of its drugs needs.

The TNCs tried to discredit the cheap drugs bought in bulk under generic names by constantly referring to their poor quality, particularly if they came from their formidable competitors in India and Eastern Europe. Such attacks were for sound commercial reasons. The TNCs had no desire to compete with small companies over prices. On the one hand, the combined use of patent and brand-name systems had shielded the TNCs from price competition, ensuring a large share and domination of the pharmaceutical market in developing countries, particularly in the production of base materials. On the other hand, while making every effort to oppose the introduction and diffusion of generics, the TNCs were at the same time moving into this field. Their adoption of this dual strategy was an attempt to safeguard their interests. Despite its espousal of the free market, the industry strongly opposed centralized bulk buying of drugs in the open market through international tenders. Such a practice would not only make it easier for the countries concerned to control existing malpractices, but would also give them more bargaining power.

It should be noted that as far back as 1959 the Sri Lankan government reduced the number of drugs available in the public sector. What provoked controversy in 1972 was the extension of this restriction to the private sector, as the director of Farbwerke Hoechst in Germany (Tiefenbacher, 1979: 412) explained:

> The pharmaceutical industry has a vital role to play in resolving the formidable task of reaching acceptable standards of health care for all. It stands ready to work for this goal with new visions and new initiatives, but only if it is permitted to serve the private market responsibly and progressively. Controls that would destroy the private market will lead inevitably to a strategic withdrawal from the third world.

The Search for a Way Forward

By the 1970s economic constraints were beginning to put stress on the government budgets of developing countries. Decreasing or static health budgets operating with diminishing resources and limited availability of convertible currency led to drugs shortages in many countries, particularly in the primary level services in rural areas. Though most developing countries had been doubling their drugs expenditures every four years, their GNPs had only been doubling every 16 years (Piachaud, 1980). With demand exceeding resources, the problems facing developing countries were most certainly going to worsen.

Faced with the impossible task of distributing their meagre financial and technical resources, reducing the costs of drugs became a matter of national concern for nearly all developing countries. Several governments (for example, India, Kenya and Tanzania) had committed themselves on independence to providing medical services for all. As Korn (1984: 34) put it, a reliable supply of drugs is 'a political stabilizer.... The politicians are aware that if drugs supplies fail, the government is in danger.'

The search for new policies began to break national boundaries. The crisis in pharmaceuticals was a global one and the safe and equitable use of medicines called for an international response. The third world had forced the debate into the international arena. For example, the Fifth Non-Aligned Conference in Colombo (in 1976) adopted resolution number 25 on cooperation among developing countries in the production, procurement and distribution of pharmaceuticals and invited the assistance of relevant international organizations (UNCTAD, 1982a: 41-57). It drew upon the conclusions of an UNCTAD study entitled *Major Issues in the Transfer of Technology in Developing Countries: A Case Study of the Pharmaceutical Industry* (UNCTAD, 1975) and endorsed the proposals put forward by the Group of Experts on Pharmaceuticals convened by the Action Programme for Economic Cooperation (APEC) in Georgetown, Guyana in 1976.

The growing debate about the activities of TNCs in developing countries (Heller, 1977), along with concerns about developing the local manufacturing industries of these countries, the rate of transfer of technology from the north to the south and the determination to make available essential drugs to the poor majorities in the developing world, have increasingly involved the various branches of the UN, especially WHO, the United Nations Conference on Trade and Development (UNCTAD), the United Nations Industrial Development Organization (UNIDO), and the United Nations Children's Fund (UNICEF). Let us turn to some of these UN initiatives.

The World Health Organization

From as early as the first WHA, in 1948, WHO had an explicit mandate to work in the area of pharmaceutical products. Until the early 1970s, however, its concern with medicines was essentially an attempt to harmonize drugs standards in international commerce; it confined itself to imposing quality controls over the chemical and physical properties of drugs (Stenzl, 1981). The thalidomide disaster in 1961 forced WHO to focus on drugs safety and efficacy, setting up in 1963 an information scheme on adverse drugs reactions. A certification scheme on 'good practices in the manufacture and quality control of drugs' was adopted in 1969. A couple of resolutions (1952, 1963) warned against inappropriate advertising of drugs and, in 1968, WHO published *Ethical and Scientific Criteria for Pharmaceutical Advertising*. It was not, however, until the mid-1970s that a more comprehensive strategy was adopted as part of a change in health policy in its broadest sense.

This was a period of substantial change in policy. In the 1970s critics of former development theories, which had emphasized the concept of modernization through investment in the physical elements of national growth (industry, roads, dams), drew attention to the relative neglect of the social aspects of development and to the imbalances in the benefits of growth. As a result attention turned to equity and to redistributive policies as a means of redressing the worst inequalities between groups. The international agencies translated some of this debate into policy. In 1974 the International Labour Office promoted the basic needs approach and, at the same time, the director-general of WHO, Mahler, introduced a broad change of policy towards improving basic health services and coverage, especially in neglected rural and peri-urban populations. By the mid- to late 1970s WHO's shift in policy had been enunciated through its promotion of the idea of Health For All by the Year 2000, to be achieved through the Primary Health Care (PHC) approach. At the PHC conference in Alma Ata in 1978, the role of medicines in PHC was recognized and essential drugs became one of the eight basic components of PHC. 'While medicinal products alone are not sufficient to provide adequate health care, they do play an important role in protecting, maintaining and restoring health of the people; [drugs are] essential tools for health care and for the improvement of the quality of life' (WHO, 1978: 5).

WHO's concern with the wider social and economic issues underlying the availability of medicines thus paralleled an overall trend within the organization to move away from a mainly technical approach focusing on the eradication of specific diseases, to a more comprehensive health policy (Walt and Rifkin, 1981). To some extent, this shift in policy was a reaction to the demands articulated by the growing membership of the newly independent developing countries within WHO (Lunde, 1984: 23). These pressures prompted WHO to review what were safe, cost effective and affordable drugs, particularly for conditions of major significance in the third world. The concept of essential drugs was introduced in 1975. Essential drugs were defined by WHO (1975) as 'those considered to be of utmost importance and hence basic, indispensable, and necessary for the health needs of the population. They should be available at all times, in the proper dosage forms, to all segments of society.'

To make this concept more specific, in 1977 WHO went on to prepare a model list of essential drugs, including about 200 generic drugs and vaccines (WHO, 1977). Most of them were no longer protected by patent rights and were known to be therapeutically effective. The notion of a limited formulary of drugs existed long before WHO officially adopted the concept of essential drugs, but it succeeded in promoting these ideas on a global level. The experiences of the Nordic countries were very helpful during the initial phase of setting criteria for determining the quality of drugs and laying down guidelines on the information and use of drugs (Lunde, 1984). There was also some exchange of experiences between African, Asian and Latin-American countries that had reduced drugs costs through a number of different restrictive drugs policies (Mamdani and Walker, 1985). As early as 1959 Sri Lanka, for example, had successfully established a formulary based on some 500 drugs in the public sector, which it extended to the private sector in 1972. Papua New Guinea, on the other hand, had introduced an essential drugs policy as early as the 1950s. National lists of essential drugs had been established by Cuba in 1963 and Mozambique in 1977. Peru had introduced a limited list of drugs for the public sector in 1971. In addition, hospital formularies were widely being used in the US (Collier and Foster, 1985). Furthermore, WHO and UNICEF had been using restrictive lists of drugs in supplying countries and in assistance programmes long before the 1970s.

The direction taken by WHO policy since the early 1960s is a good illustration of how perspectives on medicines have changed in the international community and of how policies develop within the system. In focusing on the concept of essential drugs with a view to influencing domestic policy in the third world, WHO took an important step in the launching of a new campaign on pharmaceuticals. Global social and political circumstances, particularly the emergence of an international consumers' movement in the 1970s, created a favourable environment for its acceptance. The report to the WHA in 1975 by WHO's director-general, Halfden Mahler, identified national drugs policies as a top priority for developing countries. The development of policy in WHO is described in Chapter 2.

Cooperation with other UN Agencies

UNCTAD and UNIDO were established during the 1960s in the wake of the UN's increasing preoccupation with the problems generated by the growth of technology, of large TNCs and the increasing demands of the third world for technical assistance and the transfer of technology. Both UN organizations conducted several studies on the pharmaceutical trade and its relevance to future policies. They also promoted the local production of drugs and trade in developing countries. UNCTAD attempted to negotiate a new international agreement to transfer drugs production technology to developing countries and UNIDO focused on advancing the local production of drugs in developing countries.

An UNCTAD report (UNCTAD, 1975) highlighted the vulnerability of the third world and the pressing need for coordinated policies on health planning in general. 'The leading drugs companies possess an exceedingly high degree of market power,' wrote Sanjay Lall, who went on to criticize the excessive profits made by transnational pharmaceutical companies in their trade with the third world (UNIDO, 1978). UNCTAD's policy gradually shifted towards working closely with individual governments and, at the regional level, towards assisting with the formulation and adoption of new drugs policies. It supported the use of generic names and advocated bulk purchasing by competitive tender, as well as less restrictive terms for the transfer of essential drugs technology to developing countries. Realizing that the smaller developing countries were in no position to start producing bulk pharmaceutical chemicals on their own account, UNCTAD recommended the formation of Cooperative Pharmaceutical Production and Technology Centres (COPPTECS) on a regional basis. Their objectives would be to facilitate the coordination of regional policy, to exchange information, to pool procurement and to set up local production. Efforts to promote cooperation in the pharmaceutical sector had been pursued most actively in the Caribbean region. Meanwhile, successful initiatives for cooperative joint activities were already in progress in some other sub-regions (UNCTAD, 1982a; Balasubramanium, 1983: 283-5; Mamdani and Walker, 1985). In 1971 the ministers of health for the Andean region, i.e. Bolivia, Chile (which subsequently opted out), Colombia, Ecuador, Peru and Venezuela, signed the Hipolito Unani Agreement. The Arab Company for Drug Industries and Medical Appliances (ACDIMA) was established in 1970.

UNIDO also started to widen its considerations and a tentative list of essential drugs was prepared at the 1975 International Consultation Meeting in the Field of Pharmaceutical Industries in Budapest. It seems, however, that this list was never used or published. Reports of the Second Panel of Experts on the Pharmaceutical Industries in 1978 (ID/WG 267/1) noted that medicines, produced or imported, have to be 'related to prevailing disease patterns and economic conditions of the country' (Stenzl, 1981: 222). Within this context, UNIDO's Second General Conference looked at the possibility of promoting an industrialization policy that would serve the basic needs of developing countries and, accordingly, set a very ambitious target: by the year 2000, 25 per cent of the world's pharmaceuticals should be produced in these countries (UNIDO, 1975). Since the third world produced only 11.4 per cent of all drugs in 1977, if the overall growth in world production is taken into consideration, it would need to increase its output sixfold (Muller, 1982). Nevertheless, from 1976 onwards, UNIDO concentrated on conducting feasibility studies and giving technical assistance to the numerous countries trying to start up local production of finished essential drugs. UNIDO was also involved in projects to establish the bulk production of drugs using multi-purpose plants. It encouraged the use of generics in all its projects and promoted the idea that groups of developing countries engage in cooperative production (UNIDO, 1978).

UNICEF had always played a role in supplying basic drugs and vaccines to organizations such as WHO, as well as directly to country programmes, through its supplies division (formerly UNIPAC) in Copenhagen. However, it was not until the 1981 liaison meeting of the Joint Committee on Health Policy (JCHP), the official body that links WHO and UNICEF, that UNICEF became officially involved in the essential drugs concept as such (LSHTM/KIT, 1989: 23). One of its main aims was to establish a group bulk purchasing scheme with a view to making essential drugs available to developing countries at low prices.

A Coordinated UN Response

Between 1976 and 1979 numerous inter-governmental meetings requested specific studies and actions from UN bodies. The problem of defining appropriate policies was discussed at the meeting of the non-aligned countries and at the Group of 77's conference on Economic Cooperation among Developing Countries, both of which were held in 1976. The subject was again raised at the Sixth Non-Aligned Conference in Havana in 1979. Resolution 8 on cooperation among developing countries in the pharmaceutical field was adopted and the conference formally endorsed the 27 recommendations (contained in the interregional mission's report entitled *Pharmaceuticals in the Developing World: Policies on Drugs, Trade and Production*) for action by developing countries (UNDP, 1979). In addition to providing broad directives for creating national policies and cooperative action among developing countries, these resolutions drew attention to the importance of new initiatives in the pharmaceutical sector, which would enable developing countries to achieve national and collective self-reliance in this vital area. They called for the establishment of regional pharmaceutical centres and stressed the part to be played by relevant UN organizations, such as UNCTAD, UNIDO, the United Nations Development Programme (UNDP) and WHO, in assisting developing countries achieve the objectives they had outlined. From 1975 onwards, pharmaceutical policies were regularly discussed at meetings and the need for an integrated approach to their development was identified.

In response to this need, UNCTAD, WHO, UNIDO, the UN Department of Technical Cooperation for Development and the UN Action Programme for Economic Cooperation among Non-Aligned and Other Developing Countries established a special Task Force on pharmaceuticals (Patel, 1983; Helling-Borda, 1983). This Task Force prepared a project entitled Economic and Technical Cooperation among Developing Countries in the Pharmaceutical Sector, which the UNDP then approved for funding. It also organized an interregional mission, which visited several developing countries. The ensuing report, *Pharmaceuticals in the Developing World: Policies on Drugs, Trade and Production*, which was the result of a cooperative effort by several of the Task Force's bodies (UNDP, 1979), provided the first major review of the kinds of problems faced by the third world in trying to ensure the availability of adequate supplies of appropriate drugs at a cost the majority of third world populations would be able to afford. It formed the basis for the new policies developing countries subsequently adopted. It was thus not until 1978 that an explicit and coordinated strategy on drugs policies emerged. Within the UN a rough division of labour had evolved: trade and technology (UNCTAD), health (WHO) and industry (UNIDO). For the first time these three main UN bodies worked together to determine what kinds of policies on pharmaceuticals would be adopted by developing countries.

The Task Force stressed the need for comprehensive drugs policies to ensure that everyone in the developing countries had access to essential drugs at reasonable cost. It called for the establishment within the following two years of three to six regional cooperative and pharmaceutical production centres and three to six formulation plants in developing countries (UNDP, 1979). To this end it recommended the adoption of national lists of essential drugs by generic names. These lists were to be prepared on the basis of the health needs of developing countries, taking into account the criteria and the revised model list of essential drugs as identified by the WHO Expert Committee in its second report. The Task Force's recommendations, adopted in 1979 by the Sixth Summit Conference of Non-Aligned Countries in Havana, served as the main lines of policy at the national, regional and international levels.

The next initiative was in 1980 when UNCTAD published its study, *Technology Policies and Planning for the Pharmaceutical Sector in the Developing Countries* (UNCTAD, 1980a). The report discussed in some detail the main considerations developing countries would have to take into account in planning the pharmaceutical sector. It also outlined the main phases involved in starting to produce pharmaceuticals nationally and in creating the needed technological capability.

The activities of the various UN agencies in the pharmaceutical field, between 1975 and 1981, paved the way for the establishment of a WHO Action Programme on Essential Drugs (APED) in February 1981. The basic issue was the availability of low cost, good quality essential drugs for the poor majorities in developing countries. Whether the solution lay in developing local industry or in purchasing finished drugs through international tendering, the UN had managed to develop a coordinated strategy in which all its concerned branches had a potential role to play. Whereas UNIDO and UNCTAD concentrated on countries with sufficient development to make local production and technology transfer realistic priorities, WHO directed its attention to rationalizing drugs policies in countries where the need was greatest. Its initial strategy was to improve procurement, storage and distribution of drugs. Setting APED up as a specialized unit within WHO consolidated WHO's leadership role in this field within the UN.

The Industry's Response

The large number of international meetings which took place in the 1970s and which were specifically concerned with obtaining inexpensive drugs and developing local industry led to fierce debates between the unequal and powerful interests of the pharmaceutical industry, governments, national pharmaceutical companies, UN agencies and non-governmental organizations. Two issues were at the crux of the problem: what relationship should exist between public and private sectors in achieving the stated goals, and should the essential drugs concept be a global one or be applied only to developing countries. These issues, in turn, touched on the fundamental value judgements and material interests of individuals, organizations, industries and governments.

The transnational pharmaceutical industry resisted international attempts to coordinate and promote national drugs policies in favour of essential drugs. From simply fending off their critics they moved towards actively launching campaigns to win the strategic ground. Their reaction is detailed in Chapter 3. One needs to put their response into context, however, to understand why the industry saw a change in pharmaceutical policy as a threat.

By the 1970s the pharmaceutical industry had changed considerably since its inception. Beginning with the discovery of the so-called wonder drugs (the sulphonamides in the 1930s and penicillin in the 1940s), the industry went on to develop technologies to manufacture and market the new medicines in large quantities. The initial patents granted to pharmaceutical manufacturers gave them a 17-year monopoly privilege over their innovations.

Between the 1930s and 1950s the industry underwent huge changes. The first drugs companies were relatively small, making and selling a complete range of medicines. By the 1950s they were increasingly specializing in particular products, adding research to their manufacturing capabilities. Their products were protected by patents, promoted by brand names and usually purchased through doctors' prescriptions rather than directly from the pharmacist. By the early 1960s firms were becoming increasingly transnational, with sales, production and even research carried out by affiliates located in countries outside the domicile of the original parent company.

In this same period governments introduced a more stringent regulation of drugs and research and development costs rose. By the early 1970s it was evident that the total number of new drugs approved for commercial use had dropped considerably. In the US this was from an annual average of 56 between 1950 and 1960, to 17 for the period 1961 to 1970 (UNCTC, 1979). Thus, by the 1970s the pharmaceutical industry was facing some difficulties. First, there was a spate of criticism about the double standards in its marketing and promotion practices; second, it was clear that there was a decline in the rate of innovation of pharmaceutical products; and third, by the mid-1970s it was anticipated that a large number of patents for the widely prescribed drugs that had been developed in the 1940s, 1950s and early 1960s would be expiring and the financial significance of this was creating concern. According to one estimate, patents on 104 of the 200 top selling branded drugs in the US in 1974 were due to expire in 1980 (UNCTC, 1979). Finally, there were national pressures on pharmaceutical prices. The establishment from the 1950s onwards of national health systems in a number of countries in the industrialized world had meant that governments had become the principal buyers of drugs. This created a heightened awareness of international price differences for medicines and, by 1975, several countries had introduced formal controls over drugs pricing. In an unprecedented move, some European countries took legal action against Hoffman-La Roche for allegedly over-pricing two of its major products, Librium and Valium (UNCTC, 1979).

Given this scenario, it is hardly surprising that the industry was initially antagonistic to a policy it believed was attempting to curtail its freedom of action in the production and marketing of drugs. Through the organization that represented companies at the international level, the International Federation of Pharmaceutical Manufacturers Associations (IFPMA), it lobbied national governments and international organizations to express its disapproval of the essential drugs concept launched by WHO. It declared it was 'completely unacceptable to the pharmaceutical industry' (SCRIP, 1977: 23).

Conclusion

This chapter has given an overview of the factors leading to changes in pharmaceutical policy in the late 1970s. Complex economic, political and ethical issues led to a series of changes, which resulted in some rationalization of pharmaceutical policy, though important issues were deliberately eschewed because of both the political sensitivities they incurred and the desire of many national governments and international organizations to avoid confrontation. Thus, though there is provision to develop and maintain standards for the international trade in medicinal drugs according to Article 21 of WHO's constitution, 'it is believed never to have been used' (Medawar, 1985). Whilst it is the prerogative of national governments to make decisions about regulating pharmaceuticals, the experiences of a number of developing countries during the 1960s and 1970s clearly showed that independent attempts to regulate the activities of TNCs are often futile. Conflicts of interest between the third world and TNCs tend to be greatest in the area of pharmaceutical production. Egypt pursued the path of nationalization to promote its domestic pharmaceutical industry. Argentina depended mainly on market forces with some government help. Brazil, India and Mexico, however, embraced an intermediate strategy. They proceeded to encourage the growth of local enterprises (both private and public) on the one hand, while increasing the degree of regulation of foreign firms on the other. Their experiences have demonstrated the futility of trying to regulate the activities of the TNCs (UNESC, 1981: 4): the market shares of foreign firms remain very high, ranging from 70 per cent in India to 88 per cent in Brazil.

The themes emerging from this overview suggest that developing countries themselves played an important role in pushing for a change in policy. Some did this through rationalizing a drugs policy at the national level, partly out of financial exigency, partly out of ethical consideration. In lobbying for change in the 1970s, they also became an increasingly important force in international organizations and international policy groupings. The third world had a particular ally in Halfdan Mahler and, when he became director-general of WHO in 1973, he orchestrated a change in health policy which focused on the needs of the third world. The call for Health For All by the Year 2000 and the launching of the PHC approach legitimated and provided the push towards a more rational pharmaceutical policy.

While WHO was by no means the only UN agency involved in rethinking pharmaceutical policy, it was clear that by the mid-1970s it was taking the leading role in promoting a change in policy. In Chapter 2 we look at how policy developed within the organization and at how a broad-based policy was turned into an operational plan which developing countries could implement.

References

Agarwal, A. (1978) *Drugs and the third world* . London: Earthscan

Anonymous (1970) 'The pharmaceutical industry in India'. *Science Today*, November, 21-5

Balasubramanium, K. (1983) 'The main lines of cooperation among developing countries in pharmaceuticals'. In S.J. Patel (ed.), q.v.

Bangladesh, Ministry of Health (1977) *Country health programming, Bangladesh: Programme proposal*. Dacca: MOH

Basch, P.F. (1990) *Textbook of international health*. New York and Oxford: Oxford University Press

Capo, L.R. (1983) 'International drug procurement and market intelligence: Cuba'. In S.J. Patel (ed.), q.v., 217-22

Chetley, A. and D. Gilbert (1986) *Problem drugs, section 1B (Hydroxyquinolines)*. The Hague: Health Action International

Collier, J. (1985) 'Licensing and provision of medicines in the United Kingdom: an appraisal'. *The Lancet*, 2 (8451), 377-81

Collier, J. and J. Foster (1985) 'Management of a restricted drugs policy in hospital: The first five years' experience'. *The Lancet*, 1, 331-3

Dukes, M.N.G. (1985) *The effects of drug regulation*. Lancaster: MTP Press

Fajnzylber, F. (1971) Quoted in T. Heller (1977), q.v.

Galal, E.E. (1983) 'National production of drugs: Egypt'. In S.J. Patel (ed.) q.v.

George, S. (1990) *Ill fares the land*. London: Penguin Group

Heller, T. (1977) *Poor health, rich profits. Multinational drug companies and the third world* . Nottingham: Bertrand Russell Peace Foundation Ltd.

Helling-Borda, M. (1983) *The essential drugs concept and its implementation. Health in developing countries* . International colloquium organized by the Royal Academy of Medicine of Belgium, 28-29 October, 169-86

Herxheimer, A. (1984) 'Immortality for old drugs?' *The Lancet*, 2, 1460-1

Kay, D.A. (1976) *The international regulation of pharmaceutical drugs*. A report to the National Science Foundation on the application of international regulatory techniques to scientific/technical problems. Washington DC: The American Society of International Law

Korn, J. (1984) 'Eastern Africa: Perspectives of drug usage'. *Danish Medical Bulletin*, 31 (1)

Lall, S. (1979) 'Problems of distribution, availability and utilization of agents in developing countries: An Asian perspective'. In *Pharmaceuticals for developing countries: Conference proceedings*. Washington DC: National Academy of Sciences

Lall, S. and S. Bibile (1978) 'The political economy of controlling trans-nationals and pharmaceutical industry in Sri Lanka 1972-76'. *International Journal of Health Services*, 8, 299-328

Lauridsen, E. (1984) 'The World Health Organization Action Programme on Essential Drugs'. *Danish Medical Bulletin*, 31 (1)

Lunde, P.K.M. (1982) 'Restricted drug formularies in Nordic and developing countries'. Paper presented at Management Centre Europe Conference No. 5470-66, PHARMA 82, 28-30 June, Geneva

———————— (1984) 'WHO's programme on essential drugs: background, implementation, present state, and prospectives'. *Danish Medical Bulletin*, 31 (1)

Lunde, P.K.M., C.K. Maitai and M. Mamdani (1989) *Kenya Country study*. Evaluation of WHO's Action Programme on Essential Drugs, LSHTM/KIT

LSHTM/KIT (1989) *An evaluation of WHO's Action Programme on Essential Drugs*. Submitted to the Management Advisory Committee of APED, London and Amsterdam: LSHTM and KIT

Mamdani, M. and G. Walker (1985) *Essential drugs and developing countries*. EPC publication no. 8, London: LSHTM

Marzagao, M. and M. Segall (1983) 'Drug selection: Mozambique'. In S.J. Patel (ed.), q.v., 205-16

Medawar, C. (1984) *Drugs and world health*. The Hague: IOCU

———————— (1985) 'International regulation of the supply and use of pharmaceuticals'. *Development Dialogue*, 2, 15-37

Melrose, D. (1982) *Bitter pills: Medicines and the third world poor*. Oxford: OXFAM

Muller, M. (1982) *The health of nations: A north-south investigation*. London: Faber and Faber Ltd.

Patel, S.J. (ed.) (1983) *Pharmaceuticals and health in the third world*. Oxford: Pergamon Press

Piachaud, D. (1980) 'Medicines and the third world'. *Social Science and Medicine*, 14C, 183-9

SCRIP (1977) *World Pharmaceutical News*. 259, Richmond: PJB Publications Ltd.

———————— (1981) *World Pharmaceutical News*. Richmond: PJB Publications Ltd., 4 March

Silverman, M. (1976) *The drugging of the Americas*. Berkeley: University of California Press

Stenzl, C. (1981) 'The role of international organizations in medicines policy'. In C. Blum, Herxheimer, Stenzl and Woodcock (eds) *Pharmaceuticals and health policy*, London: Croom Helm

Teeling-Smith, G. (1977) Director, Office of Health Economics, quoted in the *New Internationalist*, 50, April, 13

Tiefenbacher, M.P. (1979) 'Panel presentations'. *Pharmaceuticals for developing countries: Conference proceedings*, Washington DC: National Academy of Sciences

UNCTAD (1975) *Major issues in transfer of technology to developing countries : A case study of the pharmaceutical industry*. TD/B/C.6/4, Geneva: UN

———————— (1977) *Case studies in the transfer of technology*. New York: UN

———————— (1980) *Technology policies in the pharmaceutical sector in Cuba*. UNCTAD/TT/33, New York: UN

———————— (1980a) *Technology policies and planning for the pharmaceutical sector in the developing countries*. TD/B/C.6/56, New York: UN

———————— (1982) *Technology policies in the pharmaceutical sector in Costa Rica*. UNCTAD/TT/37, New York: UN

———————— (1982a) *Guidelines on technology issues in the pharmaceutical sector in the developing countries*. UNCTAD/TT/49, New York: UN

UNCTC (1979) *Transnational corporations and the pharmaceutical industry*. ST/CTC/9. New York: UN

———————— (1984) *Transnational corporations in the pharmaceutical industry of developing countries*. New York: UN

UNDP (1979) *Pharmaceuticals in the developing world: Policies on drugs, trade and production*. INT/009/A/01/99, New York: UNDP

UNESC (1981) *Transnational corporations in the pharmaceutical industry of developing countries: Report of the Secretariat*. E/C.10/85. New York: UN

UNIDO (1975) *Lima Declaration*. ID/Conf 3/31, Vienna: UNIDO

———————— (1978) *Growth of the pharmaceutical industry in developing countries: problems and prospects*. Study prepared by Lall in cooperation with the UNIDO Secretariat. ID/204. Vienna: UNIDO

———————— (1980) *Global study of the pharmaceutical industry*. ID/WG.3-31/6, Vienna: UNIDO

Walt, G. and S. Rifkin (1981) *The PHC approach in developing countries*. London: Ross Institute Publications, LSHTM

WHO (1975) *Prophylactic and therapeutic substances*. A22/11, Geneva: WHO

———————— (1977) *The selection of essential drugs*. Geneva: WHO

———————— (1977a) *Surveillance for the prevention and control of health hazards due to antibiotic-resistant enterobacteria*. Technical Report Series No. 624. Geneva: WHO

———————— (1978) *Thirty-first World Health Assembly. Background document for references and use at the technical discussions on national policies and practices in regard to medicinal products, and related international problems*. A31/Technical Discussions/1, Geneva: WHO

———————— (1984) *Action Programme on Essential Drugs and Vaccines: Progress report by the Executive Board Ad Hoc Committee on drug policies.* WHO/DAP/84.4, Geneva: WHO
———————— (1988) *The world drug situation.* Geneva: WHO
Wickremasinghe, S. and S. Bibile (1971) 'The management of pharmaceuticals in Ceylon'. *British Medical Journal*, 3, September
World Bank (1975) *Health Sector Policy Paper.* Washington: World Bank
Yudkin, J.S. (1980) 'The economics of pharmaceutical supply in Tanzania'. *International Journal of Health Services*, 10, 455-77

2

Formulating An Essential Drugs Policy: WHO's Role

Gill Walt and Jan Willem Harnmeijer

Until the mid-1970s WHO's role in pharmaceuticals was confined to dealing with technical matters concerned with efficacy and standards in drugs control. From 1975 onwards, however, this changed and WHO took over from the other UN agencies, UNCTAD and UNIDO, in becoming far more involved in actually helping countries develop their own national pharmaceutical policies.

In this chapter we attempt to explore this process largely in relation to questions of policy formulation. Who initiated and executed the policy? Who resisted the process of change? To what extent was the development of policy influenced by the roles of different individuals or groups? What changes occurred as a result of this process?

To understand how policies are made within WHO, it is necessary to know something about the organization's structure and policy processes.

WHO's Structure and Policy Processes

WHO, which is an agency specializing in health, forms part of the UN system. It consists of three constituent bodies: the World Health Assembly (WHA), the Executive Board (EB) and the Secretariat. The WHA meets annually (in May) and is attended by delegations from the Ministries of Health of all member states, as well as representatives from other international bodies and non-governmental organizations. The WHA's main tasks are to approve the biennial programme and budget and make major policy decisions. It is, in theory, the organization's highest policy-making body controlled by member states and it instructs the Secretariat to carry out its wishes. In practice, however, its control over policy is illusory. The WHA meets only once a year and the EB basically decides what will appear on the agenda. The occasional issue might become subject to corridor politics (certain delegations lobbying others to take a particular point of view), but this was relatively unusual at WHO assemblies until the 1980s, though common in other UN agencies. For an example, see Hushang (1982, Chapter 9) on the International Labour Office (ILO). In the early 1980s, however, WHO became subject to greater lobbying and controversy, with member delegations at the WHA being openly lobbied on a number of different issues. In a few cases this had some effect on policies strongly supported by the Secretariat. A good example of this, which is described in more detail in Chapter 3, was the action in 1981 to commit WHO to an international code on the marketing of breast milk substitutes (Sikkink, 1986).

The EB consists of 31 technically qualified health specialists, each of whom is appointed by designated member states and elected by the WHA. It meets twice yearly, normally in January and just after the WHA. As an executive organ, acting on behalf of the membership of WHO, it prepares the WHA's agenda and submits the general programme of work to it.

The Secretariat, with the director-general as its technical and administrative head, comprises the whole staff: in the headquarters in Geneva, in the six regional offices and working as WHO representatives in various countries. The six regional offices are responsible for formulating policies of a regional character; they have their own planning and biennial budget cycle, which feeds into the EB meetings in Geneva. The regions are Africa (AFRO); the Eastern Mediterranean (EMRO); Europe (EURO); the Americas (PAHO); South-East Asia (SEARO); and the Western Pacific (WPRO).

The director-general and the six regional directors are the only staff specified in WHO's constitution. It is left to the director-general's discretion to establish a staff in accordance with the organization's needs and budget. Understanding the position of the director-general is thus a key to understanding policy within WHO. As the only elected member of the Secretariat, he (all director-generals of WHO have been male) has the power to appoint everyone else at top decision-making levels. Clearly he employs people whom he believes will support and agree with his policies. He has ultimate power — he controls the budget. Given the infrequent meetings of the WHA and EB, the director-general has to translate policy and put into practice the tasks assigned to the Secretariat by the WHA. He may slow down implementation or hasten it; he may interpret policy radically or conservatively.

Halfdan Mahler, who was director-general from 1973 to 1988, knew the organization well. He had worked in India as a doctor and had spent a few years at WHO's Geneva headquarters before being elected to the post. The Mahler years, which were very different from those of his predecessors, were characterized by a committed and action-oriented programme of work strongly supportive of the less developed countries. Through his promotion of primary health care (PHC) he orchestrated a revolution in health policy; essential drugs became one of the principal elements of the PHC strategy.

Getting Essential Drugs on to the Policy Agenda

The first formal indication of the need for a policy on pharmaceuticals appeared in the director-general's report to the 1975 WHA. In this report he drew attention not only to the high expenditure on drugs in both developed and developing countries, but also to the myriad of unethical and sometimes illegal practices associated with the distribution of drugs in developing countries. He concluded (WHO, 1975) that:

> There is an urgent need to ensure that the most essential drugs are available at a reasonable price and to stimulate research and development to produce new drugs adapted to the real health requirements of developing countries. This calls for the development of national drugs policies for the whole drug sector, linking drug requirements with health priorities in national health plans formulated within the context of social and economic development.

The report followed requests for a WHO policy on drugs from member delegations eager to ensure that essential drugs were made available at reasonable cost to those in need. Helling-Borda (1983) quotes from a typical letter arriving at WHO in the early 1970s from the chief medical officer of a developing country: 'our latest indent is 105 per cent more expensive than last year's. I need hardly say that this completely makes nonsense of our financial estimates and my government cannot, in the near future, double the money allocated for medicines.' The director-general's report covered three basic interrelated issues, namely the availability, the accessibility and the efficacy of drugs. The WHA (WHO, 1975a) endorsed the report and called on the WHO Secretariat 'to provide assistance to member states to develop national drug policies emphasizing the selection and procurement of essential drugs "at reasonable cost".' The phrase 'reasonable cost' was to engender a considerable amount of discussion over the next few years.

Until 1975 WHO had largely concentrated on the safety and efficacy of specific drugs. Only one unit within the organization had a responsibility for drugs issues, namely Pharmaceuticals (PHA), which came under the Division of Diagnostic, Prophylactic and Therapeutic Substances. Concerned largely with technical or normative functions, in the 1950s PHA produced the *International Pharmacopeia* and the international nomenclature for non-proprietary names. In the 1960s its work focused largely on the safety and efficacy of drugs and on quality control. The concern for safety and efficacy was brought to a head by the thalidomide disaster in 1962, with WHO setting up a national system to provide information on adverse drug reactions. This activity was later taken over by the Swedish Board of Health in Uppsala, but remained a WHO responsibility. The unit also developed a certification scheme to help countries ensure the quality of pharmaceutical products.

The Period of Policy Exploration: 1977-1981

Establishing the Drug Policies and Management (DPM) Unit

A new unit was created within WHO to implement the new approach to drugs policy. Called the Drug Policies and Management (DPM) unit, it came under the same Division of Diagnostic, Prophylactic and Therapeutic Substances and was, at first, staffed by two members of the PHA unit. But it grew rapidly and, by 1978, had acquired additional personnel. The first head of the unit, Dr H. Nakajima, returned to WHO headquarters in 1988 as director-general.

Establishing an Essential Drugs List

The DPM's first activity was to convene an expert committee to produce a model essential drugs list. WHO often uses 'expert committees' to help formulate policy in a number of areas. Individuals with a specific expertise are invited to a round table discussion in the Geneva headquarters of WHO and, after some deliberation, they produce a technical report which serves as WHO policy in that particular area.

The official publication of the essential drugs list in 1977 (WHO, 1977) played a critical part in promoting a new approach to drugs policy. The principal characteristics of essential drugs were defined in the preamble to the model list of drugs (WHO, 1977) as safety, efficacy, need and affordability.

> While drugs *alone* are not sufficient to provide adequate health care, they do play an important role in protecting, maintaining and restoring the health of people.... It is clear that for the optimal use of limited financial resources the available drugs must be restricted to those proven to be therapeutically effective, to have acceptable safety and to satisfy the health needs of the population. The selected drugs are here called 'essential' drugs, indicating that they are of the utmost importance and are basic, indispensable and necessary for the health needs of the population.

During the discussions of the expert committee on essential drugs, the DPM unit gathered information and planned the next stage in the development of a drugs policy. During 1975 and 1976 staff visited 25 countries in four of the six WHO regions for talks with Ministry of Health officials, doctors, pharmacists and health providers at all levels of the health service. In addition, they prepared three major meetings: a consultation on drugs policy, which included the other UN agencies involved in drugs issues (UNCTAD and UNIDO) and two regional meetings to make recommendations to the WHO Secretariat on future activities in this area.

The DPM unit also prepared a paper for WHO's 1978 WHA, at which the technical discussions were to be on drugs policy (WHO, 1978a). The paper outlined WHO's approach to the drugs issue and reviewed activities over the past three years, emphasizing problems in the less developed countries. The report highlighted technical and administrative components of drugs policies and problems with implementation and referred to possible solutions.

The main proposal was to create an *action programme on essential drugs* with the objective of (WHO, 1978a: 3):

> strengthening the national capabilities of developing countries in the selection, supply and proper use of essential drugs to meet their real health needs and in the local production and quality control, wherever feasible, of such drugs. The immediate aim of the action programme is to make essential drugs and vaccines available under favourable conditions to governments of the less developed countries in order to extend essential health care and disease control to the vast majority of the population.

It is important to note that the use of the term 'reasonable' cost, which had appeared in the first documents on drugs policy, had by 1978 been replaced by 'favourable' conditions. This reflected an ongoing discussion with the pharmaceutical industry which will be explored later.

The Action Programme on Essential Drugs (APED)

As in many organizations, the process of policy making is somewhat ponderous at WHO. The proposal to launch an *action programme on essential drugs* was endorsed at the WHA in 1978, but it took three years for the administrative structure to be set up to run the activities of the action programme.

In the three years before the new administrative structure was put in place, the DPM unit undertook a range of different activities, but these reflected interests within the unit rather than a clear programme of action. The overall idea was to improve drugs supplies to developing countries by encouraging them to produce locally. Country level activities included an ambitious study of national drugs policy in Indonesia (which focused largely on local production), joint missions with individual pharmaceutical companies to four African countries to assess the drugs supply situations there, and giving support to programmes that had already been launched under the umbrella of Technical Cooperation among the Developing Countries (TCDC). One member of the DPM staff later went off to set up a pharmaceutical company in a developing country.

Setting the Priorities: 1981-1983

In February 1981 the DPM was abolished and a new unit created. After much debate this was called the Action Programme for Essential Drugs, with the acronym DAP (Drugs Action Programme). However, though it had a new name, it was staffed by the same personnel and, as far as its activities were concerned, very little changed.

By mid-1981 there was considerable tension between DAP's staff and WHO's leadership. The members of staff were confused about whether DAP was an administrative or operational unit, a programme, a strategy, or a policy. They concentrated on producing the essential drugs list, revising the original list and encouraging countries to explore the possibilities of increasing drugs supplies by establishing local pharmaceutical production. They were at odds with the leadership's high hopes of developing broad drugs policies which would lead to increased supplies at lower costs (Mahler himself felt very strongly about this issue).

All this confusion over the essential drugs concept and the role of WHO stemmed from tensions about the nature of WHO as an international organization and the extent to which it could deal with conflict. During the 1960s and 1970s many of the UN's specialist agencies were criticized for being highly politicized (Wells, 1987; Harrod and Schrijver, 1988) and for introducing issues for debate that were irrelevant to their tasks. The US used this objection to withdraw, first from the ILO in 1978 and later (1987) from UNESCO, though many have argued that there was a strong ideological rationale behind the UK and US retreat from UNESCO (Harrod and Schrijver, 1988). WHO, however, handled similar debates with some skill and, though at several assemblies the US voted against resolutions condemning Israel's health treatment in the occupied territories, this was never used as a justification for withdrawing from the organization, as it had been in the case of UNESCO (Mingst, 1990). WHO was perceived of as a sober and technically competent organization with considerable salience for developed as well as less developed countries.

This reputation was, however, severely tested over the formulation of the new pharmaceuticals policy. The pharmaceutical industry reacted quickly and negatively to the idea of an essential drugs list and, from 1978 onwards, pursued the WHO Secretariat fairly relentlessly to put its point of view. Staff in the DPM and later DAP, some of whom had worked in the pharmaceutical industry, were put under considerable pressure by the industry.

Let us look a little more closely at WHO's dialogue with the pharmaceutical industry over this period.

The Pharmaceutical Industry

The Geneva-based International Federation of Pharmaceutical Manufacturers Associations (IFPMA), the pharmaceutical industry's main representative, actively lobbied WHO throughout the 1970s. Representing an industry with an annual turnover of roughly US$100,000 million and with member associations in 47 countries, it was an influential force to be reckoned with. WHO officially established relations with the IFPMA in 1971. In 1978 Mr Michael Peretz became its first full-time vice-president and played an active part in the dialogue over drugs with WHO.

The industry's early reaction to the essential drugs policy was extremely hostile. In addition to its initial statement that the essential drugs concept was 'completely unacceptable', the IFPMA suggested that the adoption of an essential drugs list would 'result in substandard rather than improved medical care and might well reduce health standards already attained' (SCRIP, 1977). In explaining this negative reaction, Peretz (1983) later stated that the industry was concerned that:

> if WHO was recommending a list of essential drugs it would follow that WHO was implicitly arguing that all other drugs not included in the list were non-essential. I am glad to say that WHO subsequently made it clear that this was not the case. The other industry concern was whether the model list was intended to have a universal application but again WHO has clarified this point by stating that the concept is 'directed primarily to the needs of developing countries' though they go on to say that it 'does have value in other contexts'.

With a market worth US$33,000 million in sales in the developed countries in 1976 (76 per cent of the total market), legislative restrictions on 'non-essential' products in Norway, Denmark and Holland and these countries' support of the concept was seen as a significant threat.

WHO tried to deflect antagonism by involving representatives of the industry in the development of the essential drugs list and five IFPMA representatives, including its president, were present at the consultation WHO convened to discuss a model essential drugs list in Geneva in December 1976.

The IFPMA was joined in its protests by the US Pharmaceutical Manufacturers Association (PMA). The PMA is an extremely powerful lobby in the US and, in its published objection to the essential drugs concept (PMA, 1985), argued that:

> Presently, a manufacturer who has developed a new product and satisfied the drugs registration authorities that it is safe, efficacious and of the specified quality is allowed to place it on the market in most countries. PMA contends that there should be no interference with this practice and that the imposition by an expert committee of additional and arbitrary criteria involving 'essentiality' or 'medical interest' would clearly be contrary to the public interest.

Some national associations in the other major drugs producing countries took slightly more moderate positions. For example, the Danish pharmaceutical industry did not oppose the concept of essential drugs, nor did it seriously lobby its government, which was actively supporting the concept at the WHA. The industry's initial negative reaction was gradually being replaced by a concession that the less developed countries wanted essential drugs policies and that in exceptional circumstances in the poorest countries in the world, where most drugs were imported and a serious shortage of foreign exchange existed, a policy based on essential drugs was a 'practical, even if regrettable, short term decision' (SCRIP, 1977).

But having accepted the idea of essential drugs, the industry tried to limit its applicability wherever possible. From 1977 onwards many pharmaceutical companies wrote to WHO offering to provide one or two specific drugs, which they regarded as 'essential' (or which were on the first essential drugs list), at 'favourable prices' to the poorest countries. These unilateral offers were not coordinated by the IFPMA and the DPM unit was not in a position to take advantage of them. The IFPMA's main action was to make an offer on behalf of various companies to finance and provide 25 training posts in quality control for nationals of developing countries. But since air fares were not provided, fewer places were taken up than were offered. There were also some joint missions with WHO, which the pharmaceutical companies partially financed, to identify the most important health needs and to quantify drugs requirements in particular countries. However, all this interaction between WHO and the industry resulted in little progress, though it did give the industry the benevolent image of supporting public health.

Controlling Confrontational Tactics

From the early 1980s a number of consumer groups began to press actively for changes in pharmaceutical marketing practices in the third world. This is described in detail in Chapter 3. Lively campaigns and considerable media coverage challenged the somewhat remote multinational companies and a period of sometimes intense confrontation began. This was brought, unusually, to the WHA in May 1981, just months after DAP had been established. Health Action International (HAI), a coalition of consumer, professional and development action groups from 27 countries, held its inaugural meeting in Geneva and made a strong impression at the WHA, launching a pamphlet against G.D. Searle's drug, Lomotil. Its presence and that of the International Baby Food Action Network (IBFAN), which had been actively campaigning against the infant formula industry, put the pharmaceutical industry on the defensive. IBFAN, amongst others, had been successful in lobbying for the introduction of a WHO code to regulate the promotion of infant formula breast milk substitutes in the third world. The International Code of Marketing of Breast Milk Substitutes was passed by all member states except the US, despite the active opposition of the International Council of Infant Food Industries, which represented the producers of infant formula foods (Chetley, 1986).

The pharmaceutical industry knew that a WHO code on pharmaceuticals had been mooted in the director-general's 1975 report and its anticipation of consumer groups using similar tactics against the industry led to a swift response to forestall action. The IFPMA launched its own marketing code in the autumn of 1981 (and a supplementary statement the following year), reaffirming the industry's commitment to observe and monitor the code and thereby deflecting further action.

The intense lobbying tactics of consumer groups, non-governmental organizations and the industry at the 1981 WHA was a new experience for WHO and gave it the incentive it needed to demonstrate that DAP was having an effect in countries. However, even a year after DAP had been established, action appeared slow. At the EB meeting in January 1982 some members expressed disappointment at DAP's apparent lack of effect.

The progress report to the 1982 EB suggested that a lack of funds was making it difficult to implement DAP. The regular budget was restricted, approximately US$1 million in 1980/1 and 1982/3, with the only extra-budgetary allocations being US$400,000 from France. As a result, little concrete action had been observed at the country level.

The EB members began a lengthy debate on the direction of DAP. Some expressed concern that WHO was exceeding its constitutional mandate. They argued that, while it was able to play its general coordinating role in promoting the essential drugs concept, it was unclear that it was able to provide technical support for the various complexities of the pricing, procurement, distribution and quality assurance aspects of an essential drugs policy. It was suggested that emphasis should instead be placed on motivating and facilitating countries to undertake national essential drugs policies. Some members suggested that the pharmaceutical industry could handle the more technical aspects. The basic implication though was that, while the concept on which DAP was based was relatively clear, its strategies were open to interpretation.

The relationship with the pharmaceutical industry was also on the agenda for the meeting and the IFPMA's president was invited to address the board. His criticism of WHO's failure to acknowledge the industry's support for DAP (in the shape of 200 drugs offered at favourable prices) was noted. The director-general replied that it was up to the industry to clarify such offers and make them practical so that member states could appraise the benefits available to them from the industry. Two other points of discussion were of particular concern to the industry: (a) a brief observation that DAP might apply itself to both the private and public sectors and (b) that WHO promote a marketing code.

In early 1982 the feeling of policy drift became particularly intense. DAP was still pursuing the idea of local production, despite the increasing realization that it was a policy dead end, at least in Africa. It was clear from experience in South East Asia that the complexity of transferring technology was greater than had been anticipated, that it was extremely costly and that, in the end, markets in Africa were relatively limited. Supplies of drugs had to be increased by means other than local production.

A flurry of meetings took place between WHO personnel and various interest groups, with each presenting their own (conflicting) points of view on how to improve essential drugs supplies to Africa. Numerous contacts were made with the pharmaceutical industry in an attempt to define more closely the exact terms of the industry's offer of essential drugs and to reach agreement on practical support for an essential drugs programme in one or two countries. These negotiations eventually broke down, however, over disagreements about the conditions of cooperation. The industry was insisting on a limited pilot scheme in two to five countries and with no more than six to ten drugs. Furthermore, the countries in the scheme were expected to provide trained staff to prescribe drugs to patients who needed them and to have an efficient distribution system.

Such meetings took place at the highest level of leadership within WHO. The leadership's strong commitment to DAP was evident from the many meetings it held with the industry. Its impatience with the lack of progress was also evident from the many meetings it held with DAP staff.

The final impetus for action came from outside WHO. It in fact came from the Danish International Development Agency's (DANIDA's) experience of implementing an essential drugs programme in Kenya and of proposing to assist in establishing one in Tanzania. The medical adviser to DANIDA, Dr Ernst Lauridsen, had been involved in essential drugs programmes in Afghanistan and Kenya and these had successfully guaranteed supplies of essential drugs to primary health facilities. In late 1982 WHO held a meeting with top decision-makers from DANIDA, UNICEF and Tanzania, at which it was suggested that Tanzania provide the example of a countrywide essential drugs policy, with financial support from DANIDA and with UNICEF and the Tanzanian Ministry of Health as co-executors of the programme. Soon after this Dr Lauridsen was persuaded to join WHO as programme manager of DAP, with responsibility for getting DAP operational in different countries. Any negotiations with the pharmaceutical industry fell away and DAP began to concentrate on demonstrating what an essential drugs programme might look like in a developing country.

Advocacy and Action: 1983-1988

DAP's new programme manager turned what had been a fairly conventional programme, run along orthodox WHO lines, into a far more dynamic global venture covering both essential drugs policies and practical help to the countries in question. From mid-1983 DAP channelled assistance to countries committed to introducing an overall national policy. This strategy, which included a spirited marketing of the concept, was assisted by a flexible structure and style of management and a dedicated staff, the former made possible by changes in the organizational accountability of the programme. At the end of 1983 DAP was moved from the Division of Diagnostic, Prophylactic and Therapeutic Substances to the Office of the Director-General. This move demonstrated the importance the leadership accorded to DAP and gave its programme manager direct contact with the director-general himself. The two had regular meetings in which sensitive relations with the pharmaceutical industry were discussed privately. The programme manager was able to select his own staff and soon built up a committed and energetic team. The decision to move DAP directly into the Director-General's Office was not, however, welcomed by all within WHO. DAP's programme manager was appointed at the salary level of a director (DG2), which was higher than the PHA programme manager's and some bureaucrats in WHO objected to this preferential treatment.

By 1988 the number of staff in DAP had almost doubled from nine full-time members in 1982/3 to 17 in 1988/9 (Armstrong, 1989). See Table 2.1.

Table 2.1: DAP Financial Resources (1980-9) for Global and Interregional Activities (in US$)

	1980-81	82-83	84-85	86-87	88-89	1980-89
Regular budget		1,056,000	1,142,000	1,115,600	1,323,300	4,636,900
Other sources						
Canada (CIDA)			379,332			379,332
Denmark (DANIDA)		595,238	1,165,488	2,171,411	2,667,713	7,099,850
Finland (FINNIDA)			71,318	205,572	2,615,275	2,892,165
France	400,000		24,631	90,833	27,419	542,883
Interpharma, Basle			37,879			37,879
Italy			800,500	250,000		1,050,500
Japan				50,000	100,000	150,000
Netherlands				5,601,254	4,680,017	10,281,271
Norway					453,247	453,247
Sweden (SIDA/ SAREC)			351,753	549,801	637,513	1,539,067
Switzerland			186,143	773,221	347,222	1,306,586
United Kingdom			286,692	550,264	1,072,099	1,905,055
UNHCR				20,000		20,000
UNICEF				5,000		5,000
UN Development Fund					22,600	22,600
Nigeria (Trust Fund)				629,351	1,224,349	1,853,700
Denmark (APO)			126,851	70,861	68,200	265,912
Japan (APO)		25,657				25,657
Various Institutions			750			750
Interest, adjustments and refunds			273,306	797,070	568,500	1,638,876
Miscellaneous					87	87
Total other sources	400,000	620,895	3,700,643	11,764,638	14,984,155	31,470,331
Grand total	**400,000**	**1,676,895**	**4,842,643**	**12,880,238**	**16,307,455**	**36,107,231**

Source: Action Programme on Essential Drugs and Vaccines, Progress Report, May 1989, Geneva: WHO, DAP 89.5

The increase in staff was made possible by the programme manager concentrating his initial efforts on attracting extra-budgetary resources and then using the money to build and reinforce donor confidence in DAP, thus attracting further contributions. As Table 2.1 shows, 'other sources' provided a significant increase in the number of staff taken on by DAP. In 1984/5 over 50 per cent of its budget was allocated to country support activities, which was exactly what the donors wanted to see. By 1984 donor contributions to DAP were sufficiently high for WHO's budgeting office to create a special extra-budgetary account to earn interest for DAP.

DANIDA made an initial contribution of almost US$600,000 during the 1982/3 budget period. Thus, although funds for DAP's regular budget remained relatively constant at just over US$1 million a year, extra-budgetary sources grew markedly. While for the year 1980/1 they stood at about US$400,000, by 1988/9 they had exceeded US$20 million, as shown in Table 2.2.

Table 2.2: Staffing Levels of DAP, Geneva

Year	1982/3		1984/5		1986/7		1988/9	
Fund	R	O	R	O	R	O	R	O
No.	6	3	6	3	6	9	6	11
Total	**9**		**9**		**15**		**17**	

Key: R = Regular budget; O = Other sources
Source: Armstrong (1989)

The rapid growth of DAP brought into focus the relationship between it and PHA, the other WHO unit concerned with drugs. PHA focused mainly on the technical aspects of drugs and took over the convening of the various expert committees which met to revise the original essential drugs list between 1978 and 1988. Among other things, it revised the certification scheme, produced guidelines on aspects of quality control, organized the Drug Regulatory Authorities' international conferences in Rome (1982) and Stockholm (1984) and managed a training scheme in analytical chemistry for pharmacists/chemists from developing countries, which the pharmaceutical industry funded (WHO, 1985). The concern expressed at the EB in 1984 (WHO, 1984) about the allocation of tasks between DAP and PHA was in fact less about the division of responsibilities than about inequalities in status and budget and, in 1984, PHA was moved to the Director-General's Office. PHA did not, however, seek funding from extra-budgetary sources, nor did it expand greatly in this period.

Besides raising additional funds from external sources, in 1983, as part of WHO's Global Medium-Term Plan, the new programme manager helped devise a work plan for DAP. This was produced in an atmosphere of great urgency and many of its targets relied on having an effective communications strategy, which was part of the new approach DAP introduced after

1983. Though not formally conceptualized until 1986/7, DAP's work fell into four basic areas, of which the most important was country support.

Country Support: Making Essential Drugs Available

When in 1982 the WHA asked DAP for a plan of action, it had little national experience on which to draw. Several regional offices had explored the possibility of regional drugs procurement schemes, but none had materialized. In the WPRO region a great deal of activity had focused on the potential for producing drugs locally, but not on essential drugs policies. In the EMRO region WHO and UNICEF had made situational analyses of several countries, but no concrete action had been taken. Only in the AFRO region, in Kenya, had a pilot project based on a kit system been undertaken to supply essential drugs to the national health services. This project guaranteed essential medicines for 3,000 patients at local health facilities. Packed centrally, kits of essential drugs were despatched to the periphery, reducing losses from breakage, pilferage and wastage.

The Kenyan experience cited above provided the catalyst for renewed efforts to promote essential drugs and, after discussions in Geneva, it was agreed that it would be used as an example for essential drugs promotion. A workshop was held to which officials from a range of countries in each of the WHO regions were invited. Two more workshops, one in French and one in English, were held again in 1983 to disseminate the Kenyan experience and to promote the essential drugs concept.

Tanzania offered another opportunity to promote the essential drugs concept. Facing an economic crisis and increasingly unable to provide drugs for its health service, it asked for donor support to help procure drugs and to rationalize the drugs supply system. DANIDA agreed to provide US$30 million for a project to supply essential drugs kits along the lines of the Kenyan model and UNICEF, in partnership with Tanzania's Ministry of Health, became the executing agency (Kanji et al., 1989).

In 1982 the new Bangladesh Drug (Control) Ordinance banned 1,700 drugs from production or sale and attempted to restrict drugs sales by foreign firms. WHO was taken by surprise by this move so offered no immediate endorsement. In 1983, however, DAP identified the action as proof of Bangladesh's acceptance of its programme and linked its name to it by supporting two quality control consultants for an ongoing donor aided drugs programme (Martinussen and Rifkin, 1989). Although the policy had a positive effect on the prices of generic drugs by driving them downwards and making them more accessible, the Bangladesh project was geared less towards the supply of drugs than towards the control of non-essential drugs.

Supporting countries' activities became the main basis of DAP's work in 1983. The new programme manager had explicitly set out to do this in order to increase supplies of essential drugs; the idea was to have DAP involved in one or two countries in each region to serve as a catalyst for the essential drugs concept. By 1984/5 over 50 per cent of DAP's resources were being channelled into this kind of work and a symbiotic relationship gradually evolved between providing support and technical advice to countries and using information from these countries to promote the essential drugs concept (WHO, 1984; 1987; 1988).

Advocacy and Communications

Between 1983 and 1985 DAP concentrated on the supply side of drugs, particularly their selection, procurement and distribution, and the feasibility of regularly supplying rural areas in developing countries. The three main lines of communications were with UNICEF'S supplies division (UNIPAC) to ensure the supply of essential drugs, the donors to guarantee funds, and the third world governments to advocate the concept. Most of these interactions took place informally in meetings with the EB and WHA. The Kenyan and Tanzanian programmes highlighted three further communication needs, namely training materials in the use of essential drugs, guidelines for evaluating essential drugs programmes, and some way of addressing issues related to financing. With the establishment of *The Essential Drugs Monitor* in 1985, the dissemination and promotion of the essential drugs concept became more systematic and widespread. DAP staff also wrote papers for scientific journals, gave talks to various bodies and produced audio-visual material for meetings. By the mid-1980s DAP had a much higher profile and had distanced itself from the pharmaceutical industry, with whom it now only communicated to complain about instances in which the industry's code of practice had been broken.

DAP's programme manager combined a careful selection of experienced, energetic and professional staff with opportunism and a dynamic style of management. Direct control over the budget and thus a great deal of autonomy in developing initiatives, as well as a flexible response to staff proposals and requests, led to an efficiently functioning unit with few formal planning, monitoring or communications procedures. From around 1986 funds were available and the programme manager kept a buffer sum of US$5 million aside for rapid and flexible responses to interesting initiatives.

Nairobi and the Revised Drugs Strategy

At the 1984 WHA the Nordic countries proposed a resolution for a meeting of 'experts' to discuss DAP's progress. There was some concern among activists such as HAI that, with irrational prescribing being a critical problem in many countries, the focus on *supplying* drugs had overshadowed the equally important area of *using* drugs. The resolution was passed and, soon after, preparations began for an international meeting of experts to be held the following year.

Chetley (1990) describes the machinations of planning the meeting and WHO's fears that it could severely damage the organization. The choice of Kenya as the host country was thus not only because it had an essential drugs programme for delegates to visit, but also because WHO was trying to lower its profile by holding the meeting outside Europe.

The meeting was attended by participants from governments, national drugs regulatory authorities, the pharmaceutical industry, consumer and patient organizations, health care providers, academics and representatives from other UN agencies and non-governmental organizations. Though surrounded by intrigue and controversy (Chetley, 1990), the main proceedings of the meeting were handled with discretion. Issues that had been expected to be controversial, such as WHO's role as a supranational regulatory body and its implementation of a marketing code, were controlled procedurally and the disparate group of experts agreed to support the need for governments to adopt national drugs policies based on the essential drugs concept. It was generally conceded that success in establishing the rational distribution, prescription and use of drugs depended on the political will of governments, as well as on having sound policy advice and technical assistance from WHO.

The consensus that emerged from the Nairobi conference provided the basis for a broader approach to essential drugs. The revised drugs strategy DAP produced in 1986 reiterated this need and shifted the emphasis within DAP towards concentrating more on disseminating information, while using PHA to deal with the normative aspects. This revised strategy, which the WHA ratified in 1986, provided the rationale for a shift in DAP's communications priorities. Information was now targeted towards health service providers, their teachers and members of the public, though activities for this last group were slow to develop. In 1987 an information officer was appointed to rationalize the provision and documentation of information within DAP and, in 1988, DAP produced its first comprehensive communications strategy.

While not abandoning country support, the revised drugs strategy focused on the relevance of the essential drugs concept for *both* developed and developing countries, underlining the rational use of drugs, the importance of dissemination and the universality of concern. By the mid-1980s some developed countries had introduced limited lists and generic prescribing to cut drugs costs. The essential drugs concept was beginning to move beyond being simply a developing country concern with a supply focus.

Because the revised drugs strategy implied that there would be more and increasingly complex work to undertake, the programme manager asked WHO's Management Unit to carry out a management survey for DAP. The survey, which included visits to two WHO regional offices (AFRO and EMRO), acknowledged the value of DAP's entrepreneurial management style, which reduced bureaucratic procedures to a minimum, but suggested a more systematic classification of its work and more transparent financial management. The recommendations were mostly implemented.

Though WHO's Secretariat played a critical role in developing policy on essential drugs and, later, in promoting it widely, this can only be understood within the context of its relationships with regional headquarters and UNICEF.

Disseminating the Essential Drugs Concept: WHO's Regional Offices

To varying degrees WHO's regional offices also played a part in disseminating the essential drugs concept. The six regions were established to make WHO more responsive to regional differences and to countries' needs. In each country a WHO representative would facilitate communication between the Ministry of Health, the regional office and headquarters in Geneva. Some representatives actively initiated policy dialogue, but many were relatively passive and saw their role largely as one of responding to government requests. The provision in 1983 of special budgets for regional organization decentralized much of the headquarters' work to regional and country level. This gave regional offices and WHO representatives more freedom to operate outside the direct control of the Geneva headquarters and meant that they could adjust their priorities to local situations. The member states making up each region had different social, economic and political characteristics and this also affected policy in the regional office.

EMRO was the first region to express its intention to adopt the essential drugs concept and this was introduced in 1978. The WPRO and SEARO, however, only formally adopted it as regional policy in 1981, after regional seminars on essential drugs in Colombo and Manila.

Some countries have formed special associations. For example, WPRO and SEARO help administer the pharmaceutical programme of the Association of Southeast Asian Nations (ASEAN), a group established to foster interregional cooperation in economic and social endeavours. Though cultural similarities are cited as unifying the member nations (Brunei, Indonesia, Malaysia, Singapore, the Philippines and Thailand), ASEAN members share more in terms of open market economic philosophies. Many of the countries have important pharmaceutical manufacturing industries and, despite the IFPMA code, some of these employ unscrupulous marketing practices. In terms of essential drugs this has meant an emphasis on upgrading technical skills for controlling quality and evaluating drugs, and essential drugs lists being perceived of as appropriate mainly for public sectors, which are seen to cater for the 'poorer' segments of the community. PAHO had for a long time been involved in aspects of essential drugs, but pursued the policy more vigorously after a leadership change in 1983. The Andean Pact countries (Bolivia, Colombia, Ecuador, Peru and Venezuela) have long had an agreed policy on various aspects of drugs control, but have been unable to implement it because of political instability, weak public health sectors and substantial private pharmaceutical production. Though there are now essential drugs projects in a number of countries in the PAHO region, many suffer the same constraints as the Andean countries. PAHO's capacity in the region is itself limited, as is its potential for supporting essential drugs programmes in the face of difficult debts and multinational strongholds.

The African Regional office (AFRO) produced an essential drugs list of 40 products at the end of the 1970s and, with support from both WHO headquarters and UNICEF, put a great deal of energy into pursuing the possibility of bulk purchasing. In 1983, after considering some of the complexities of purchase and delivery and after discussing the financing of such a scheme with the African Development Bank and the World Bank, the idea of a bulk procurement scheme was abandoned as not viable.

Though Kenya and Tanzania had hosted the first essential drugs programmes, DAP largely circumvented AFRO. Its programme manager did not even pay a visit to the regional office until 1986 and donors tended to ignore its wishes. For example, AFRO's choice of five countries to receive support in a US$15 million project on essential drugs was overturned. AFRO was deliberately sidestepped in this way because of its reputation for being reactive rather than proactive and for being unenthusiastic about advocating essential drugs policies. But such a view, however, was in stark contrast to the enthusiasm with which AFRO received the Bamako Initiative, which UNICEF's executive director, Dr James Grant, launched at AFRO's regional meeting in Mali in 1987. Let us now turn to relations with UNICEF.

Disseminating the Essential Drugs Concept: UNICEF

UNICEF has always played a role in supplying basic drugs and vaccines to organizations such as WHO, as well as directly to country programmes, but did not otherwise become involved in the essential drugs concept until the early 1980s.

The Joint Committee on Health Policy (JCHP), which officially links WHO and UNICEF, meets every two years and has liaison meetings twice a year. The JCHP's joint programme on essential drugs was initiated at the 1981 meeting as a response to the establishment of DAP in WHO and the development of primary health programmes at the country level. The purpose of the programme was 'to collaborate with developing countries in supporting the extension of their health care coverage through provision of essential drugs for primary health care by maximum utilization of both organizations' expertise, infrastructure and world network of ongoing activities' (WHO, 1981).

Though joint action on the essential drugs programme entailed different sorts of collaboration between WHO and UNICEF, including joint country visits to assess the drugs situation, the focus of cooperation was, from the beginning, on the procurement of drugs. Thus, one of the main aims of the WHO/UNICEF programme was to establish a group bulk purchasing scheme. The 1981 JCHP noted that 33 African countries had made concrete requests to WHO's regional office in Africa to develop such a scheme to improve the drugs supply situation and this was then given high priority for action.

Pool procurement by groups of countries (discussions had occurred in the Americas and Western Pacific as well as Africa) never materialized because of the complexity of the process, difficulties in establishing appropriate legal and commercial agreements among countries and problems in implementing the various administrative and financial mechanisms. By 1984 it was clear that pool procurement, or bulk purchasing as had been originally envisaged, was unlikely to succeed and other channels would have to be pursued.

The obvious answer was to increase the capacity of the UNICEF Packing and Assembly Centre (UNIPAC) in Copenhagen, for it was already buying large quantities of essential drugs on the world market, had long experience of shipping supplies to developing countries and had a new warehouse which gave it the ability to handle a greatly increased volume. With the establishment of the Tanzanian programme and large-scale bulk purchasing of essential drugs, UNIPAC's supply operation increased considerably. The volume of drugs handled moved from US$17 million in 1982, to US$35 million in 1985 and to US$6O million in 1986. Prices for essential drugs paid by UNICEF declined by the order of 50 to 60 per cent and this was largely through the efficient use of international competitive tendering and bulk purchasing orders (WHO, 1987a).

Having achieved a great deal on the supply and distribution side, UNICEF announced a rather different policy focus in 1987. At the AFRO regional meeting of WHO, the Bamako Initiative resolution was presented as a way of revitalizing primary health services in Africa. Basically this was a proposal that UNICEF provide essential drugs for use in primary level maternal and child health clinics *on condition* that charges be made for drugs or services, with the resulting income being spent on health workers' salaries or other aspects of building up primary health services.

Though Mahler was at the AFRO regional meeting, he did not know until just before it what James Grant meant by the 'Bamako Initiative' (personal communication). The lack of consultation over what a health-related policy was and the failure to take account of its implications for essential drugs policies affronted many at WHO and, in the period that followed the initiative, met with considerable criticism.

Attempts to answer reservations allayed neither the difficulties envisaged in its operation nor the more fundamental ethical and moral objections raised. One problem concerned charging sick people for drugs they needed and there was a great deal of uncertainty over what to charge: whether to try to recover total or partial costs of drugs, or whether to subsidize the more expensive drugs. There were a number of unpredictable factors that had apparently not received due consideration, such as governments receiving drugs at low cost (or free from donors) and selling them to their people at higher prices to cover the costs of rural health services.

Many within WHO in general and DAP in particular were concerned, not only about the feasibility of implementation, but the extent to which the initiative would undermine the essential drugs policy by, for example, encouraging irrational prescribing. It later became clear that UNICEF had not thought through many of the policy implications; in several countries certain of its aspects (for example, recovering the full costs of drugs) were changed when it was implemented.

In 1989 the JCHP heard that UNICEF's EB had agreed to let UNICEF proceed with its own support for the Bamako Initiative (US$2 million from general resources) while seeking supplementary funds (up to US$30 million) for specific country support. At UNICEF'S EB meeting donors seemed reluctant to fund the initiative as it was presented. UNICEF then set up a joint committee with WHO in Geneva, specifically to discuss policy development and the Bamako Initiative, and established close relations with AFRO to assist in its implementation. Since the announcement of the policy the emphasis on cost recovery issues has shifted and the Bamako Initiative Management Unit at UNICEF's headquarters in New York has broadened the initial policy to a much less contentious, if not less difficult, policy on PHC.

Policy Drift: 1988-1990

While many at WHO were annoyed by the Bamako Initiative, it did not engender anywhere near as much concern as the change in leadership. In 1988 Dr Mahler's term of office as director-general came to an end and, in a flurry of voting and lobbying uncertainty, Dr Nakajima became WHO's fifth director-general. He was, of course, known to DAP both in his position as the first head of the DPM unit in 1976 and as head of the WPRO.

One of Nakajima's first actions on taking office in 1988 was to take DAP and PHA out of the Director-General's Office and put them into a new DPM unit. Dr Fattorusso, who until 1979 had been director of the Division of Prophylactic, Diagnostic and Therapeutic Substances, was brought out of retirement and appointed acting director of this division. Dr Lauridsen resigned as DAP programme manager and, in mid-1989, Dr Antezana, also a member of the original DPM unit, replaced him.

With their extra bureaucratic procedures the managerial changes introduced in 1988 and 1989 imposed different working conditions on DAP's staff. For example, permission to attend conferences, give speeches and visit countries, which had previously been relatively easy to acquire from the programme manager, became more bureaucratic and permission even for the programme manager's own visits had to be obtained from the acting director of the division. On at least two occasions such permission was refused. Planned visits to the Philippines and Mexico were at first not authorized, though the visit to Mexico did eventually take place. Papers and letters were no longer sent first to the programme manager. Rumours abounded amidst considerable speculation about the extent to which the leadership would or would not continue to support the essential drugs concept and the revised drugs strategy.

Meetings of the interested parties (donors, non-governmental organizations and other UN representatives) took place in 1986, 1988 and 1989. At the meeting in May 1989 Dr Nakajima announced that the group would be restructured into a Management Advisory Committee. The position of the interested parties would be formalized and its members given the role of advising the director-general on various aspects of DAP. This restructuring made it possible for the Management Advisory Committee to monitor more closely not only DAP's activities but also its adherence to the policies defined at the WHAs. Dr Nakajima also outlined the reasons for the changes in the organizational structure affecting DAP and added (Nakajima, 1989), 'I should like to emphasize that for the Action Programme on Essential drugs this change is one of administration and not of policy. As you are aware, the Programme's goals and objectives are clearly stated in WHO's revised drug strategy and also by the 39th World Health Assembly and these, of course, remain unaltered.' Despite considerable pressure from the interested parties to focus on questions of staffing and operations, the head of the new DPM merely reiterated the organization's support for DAP. The interested parties' concern arose in part from one of the director-general's earlier speeches (Nakajima, 1988), in which he drew a distinction between the responsibilities of WHO and of its member states:

> Under the terms of its constitution, the World Health Organization is required to cooperate with governments, upon request, in strengthening health services and also to provide information, counsel and cooperation in the field of health. It is expected to furnish technical support and services, to promote research, to provide a forum for informed debate, even to examine the available options for strengthening health services. Determination of national policy, however, is the prerogative of national governments.

While this was not new, some suggested that this could be interpreted as a future shift of balance in essential drugs policy towards national government action, with WHO providing less advocacy and more technical advice.

Despite the acceptance of the essential drugs policy, the question of how far WHO should be involved in actively implementing the policy remains a source of tension. Many argue that the role of a global specialist agency such as WHO lies in its skills of coordination, facilitation and technical advice and not in implementation or action, which is the prerogative of national policy-makers. The line between these two views is often quite fine and is strongly influenced by the leadership of the organization.

Participation in the policy process and the confrontational tactics pursued by both the pharmaceutical industry and the consumer groups exacerbated the underlying tension with WHO; it was also affected by the political climate in the US, which provides 25 per cent of WHO's budget. The withholding of this submission for the years 1986 and 1987 was allegedly because the US disapproved of some of the more contentious issues of the Mahler years (the code on breast milk substitutes and many of the essential drugs issues). There was no doubt that the activities of the consumer organizations in lobbying at the international level met the approbation of the delegations from the US and the pharmaceutical industry. No director-general can afford to court the displeasure of the US for long, though it is interesting how far the radical policies pursued by WHO throughout the late 1970s and early 1980s were tolerated. As director-general, Mahler played a skilful role in pushing for policies he believed in, such as essential drugs, but keeping the more radical demands (such as to include the private sector or the industrialized countries within the essential drugs concept) at bay, to avoid all out confrontation. The new Japanese director-general is more likely to be sympathetic to the ideological stance of the US and Japan.

By mid-1990 donor frustration with the slow rate of progress in DAP and the appointment of Dr John Dunne (long time head of PHA) as director of the Division of Drug Management and Policies (DMP) had led to the withdrawal of some funds by DANIDA. Dr Dunne remained head of PHA (as well as director of the division), with Dr Antezana continuing as head of DAP. Donor dissatisfaction was exacerbated by an apparent lack of agreement within the DMP over the control of DAP's programme and budget.

Thus, though after the inertia and lack of motivation that had followed the previous programme manager's resignation, donors at the 1991 Management Committee meeting expressed some satisfaction with the consolidation of the programme, there was still concern over the lack of clarity about DAP's management structure within the DMP. Until this is clarified donor funding of DAP will be maintained at current levels. Given inflation and rising costs, a zero growth budget implies a reduction in activities on essential drugs.

This chapter has explored the policy process. In summing up, several issues stand out.

Policy on essential drugs evolved slowly and increased in scope over the years. From a relatively modest start with an essential drugs list, WHO set up an action programme which by 1988 had embraced all aspects of a national drugs policy. This expansion was made possible by skilful and professional marketing of the essential drugs concept. DAP's role as the operational arm of the programme was central to this expansion, especially after 1983.

The acceptance of the essential drugs concept a decade after its introduction is remarkable given its negative reception by the powerful pharmaceutical industry, which employed a number of stick and carrot tactics to limit essential drugs policies. WHO demonstrated diverse skills in keeping a dialogue open without losing its resolve.

In this WHO was assisted, though indirectly, by the increasingly professional consumer and non-governmental organizations that were always trying to get it to move faster and more radically than it was doing. The intense participation of the industry and consumer groups in the international policy process was a new experience, with WHO in a push-pull situation between a protective industry and a consumer lobby arguing for change.

WHO legitimated the essential drugs concept in such a way as to force the industry to examine its constituent members more closely. In the decade of the 1980s a somewhat more self-critical approach was adopted with some companies undertaking significant reforms in marketing and information practice. Through their contributions to DAP and their outspoken support for it, donor agencies in Europe, particularly the Scandinavian countries, facilitated a rapid expansion of DAP's programmes. By not demanding a rigid system of accountability for these programmes, donors both showed confidence in DAP and allowed its programme manager maximum flexibility, with both positive and negative consequences. Donor aid was a cornerstone of policy implementation. It remains to be seen whether new donors will replace present donors. It may be that the essential drugs programme will merely limit its activities to a smaller funding base, though it is possible that organizations outside WHO will continue to promote the essential drugs concept.

The director-general's move in 1983 to bring DAP directly into his own office was strategically designed to give the programme visibility, support and protection. From 1983 onwards, the move contributed to the growth of both the advocacy and technical support DAP provided under the dynamic direction of its new programme manager. In contrast, the action of the new director-general in 1988 to remove DAP from under his aegis and place it within a new DPM division can be seen as a rational decision on managerial grounds. The controversy surrounding the essential drugs concept has not, however, disappeared and, though it was managerially correct to incorporate DAP into the WHO bureaucracy, it suggested that in political terms DAP would no longer receive the support and protection previously afforded by the Director-General's Office.

There is no doubt that WHO played a critical role in getting the essential drugs concept onto the international policy agenda. The promotion of the PHC approach from the late 1970s added impetus to the concept of essential drugs, which was seen as an important component of basic PHC services. How the essential drugs concept fared once on the agenda was the result of a process influenced by many different interests, none of which WHO could afford to ignore. At the implementation stage other factors come into play and, though WHO may itself try to influence national decision-making on drugs policy, it has no regulatory powers to enforce implementation. In the end, it is the countries that decide their own drugs policies and these are discussed in Chapter 4.

References

Armstrong, J. (1989) 'The financing of WHO's Action Programme on Essential Drugs'. Unpublished background paper prepared for *An evaluation of WHO's Action Programme on Essential Drugs*, London and Amsterdam: LSHTM/KIT

Chetley, A. (1986) *The politics of babyfoods*. London: Frances Pinter

—————— (1990) *A healthy business? World health and the pharmaceutical industry*. London: Zed Books

Harrod, J. and N. Schrijver (1988) *The UN under attack*. Aldershot: Gower

Helling-Borda, M. (1983) 'Drug selection, a way to better therapy?'. *Journal of Social and Administrative Pharmacy*, 1 (3)

Hushang, A. (1982) *Politics and process in the specialized agencies of the United Nations*. Gower: Aldershot

Kanji, N., G. Munishi, G. Sterky (1989) 'Tanzania case study'. Prepared for *An evaluation of WHO's Action Programme on Essential Drugs*, London and Amsterdam: LSHTM/KIT

Martinussen, J. and S Rifkin (1989) Unpublished background paper prepared for *An evaluation of WHO's Action Programme on Essential Drugs*, London and Amsterdam: LSHTM/KIT

Mingst, K. (1990) 'The United States and the World Health Organization'. In M. Karns and K. Mingst, *The United States and multilateral institutions*, Boston: Unwin Hyman

Nakajima, H. (1988) 'Address to the 14th Assembly of the International Federation of Pharmaceutical Manufacturers Associations', Washington, 4-6 October

—————— (1989) 'Speech to the Third Meeting of Interested Parties', Geneva, 25-26 May

Peretz, S.M. (1983) 'An industry view of restricted drugs formularies'. *Journal of Social and Administrative Pharmacy*, 1 (3), 130-3

PMA (1985) *The health care consequences of restricted drug lists*, Washington: PMA leaflet

SCRIP (1977) Quoted in I. Prudencio (1988) *El econcepto del medicamento esencial*, Italy: Mario Negri Institute

Sikkink, K. (1986) 'Codes of conduct for transnational corporations: The case of the WHO/UNICEF code'. *International Organization*, 40 (4), 817-40

Wells, C. (1987) *The UN, UNESCO and the politics of knowledge*. Macmillan: London

WHO (1977) *The selection of essential drugs*. Technical Report Series, 615

WHO official documents, unpublished:

—————— (1975) A28/11
—————— (1975a) WHA 28.66
—————— (1978) A31/Technical Discussions/1
—————— (1978a) EB63/19

———————— (1981) JC23/UNICEF-WHO/81.4
———————— (1984) EB73/18
———————— (1985) PHA/85.36 Training in drug quality control
———————— (1987) DAP 87.8
———————— (1987a) JC26/UNICEF-WHO/87.7
———————— (1988) EB 81/25

3

Consumers versus Producers: Power Play Behind the Scenes

Anita Hardon

Introduction

In Chapter 2 we looked at WHO's role in formulating an essential drugs policy to increase the availability of safe, effective and affordable drugs in the third world. In this chapter we discuss the controversies surrounding WHO's activities which, according to Reich (1987), 'have been criticized by the pharmaceutical industry, by conservative critics and by the Reagan administration, all seeking to protect the private market from the restrictions of national formularies, constrain the WHO programme to the public health system in poor countries, and keep WHO from becoming an international regulatory agency.' Consumer groups sought to push WHO to accept the principles of real medical need, significant therapeutic value and acceptably safe and satisfactory value for money as applicable to private as well as public health systems and to rich as well as poor countries.

At the international level the controversies were most apparent in the recurrent debates at the World Health Assemblies (WHAs), when the progress reports and plans of the Action Programme on Essential Drugs (DAP) were discussed and resolutions debated. (At the national level controversies emerged when governments took the initiative in developing essential drugs policies. This is discussed in Chapter 4.) The two main non-governmental actors at the WHAs were the International Federation of Pharmaceutical Manufacturers Associations (IFPMA) (with member associations in 47 countries) and Health Action International (HAI), an international coalition of some 50 non-governmental organizations (NGOs) from 27 countries, active in public interest issues and the field of health and pharmaceuticals. IFPMA and HAI sought alliances with friendly government delegations to pursue their interests.

This chapter illustrates the power play of consumers and producers behind the scenes of the WHAs, focusing on the lobbying efforts of IFPMA and HAI, their alliances with various government delegations and the overall impact of these activities on WHO's policy formulating process, as determined by resolutions adopted by the WHA.

The Early Years of DAP

Criticism of the transnational pharmaceutical industry began to increase in the 1970s when consumer organizations and other public interest groups started to act as 'watch dogs' of corporate activities.

When WHO adopted the 'breast milk substitutes' code in 1981, the transnational health-related industries became concerned about the possibility of WHO trying to regulate and monitor their private sector activities. The code, or fear of regulation, determined the course of much of the pharmaceutical industry's lobbying in WHO for the years ahead. Because of this we briefly discuss the code's history, focusing on the power play between consumers, advocates and producers.

The code was the eventual result of nearly a decade of campaigning against the promotion of powdered baby milk and the whole concept of artificial infant feeding, which were having negative effects on breast feeding rates and subsequently on infant health. The International Baby Food Action Network (IBFAN) stressed that 'breast is best' because it protects babies against illnesses, improves emotional and psychological bonding between mother and child, inhibits ovulation in the mother which helps to increase the interval between births of children and costs less than artificial feeding.

As early as the mid-1960s pediatricians were beginning to sound the first warning bells against the growing trend towards bottle feeding in the third world and the effect it was having on infant mortality and malnutrition. In an article titled 'Commerciogenic Malnutrition', Jelliffe (1971) called on food companies to enter into a voluntary dialogue with concerned medical practitioners in an attempt to restrict their activities. The dialogue bore little fruit. In the early 1970s the debate intensified when the *New Internationalist* published articles on the issue and War on Want, a UK based public interest group, published *The Baby Killer*, which presented the issue to a wider public in readable manner. *The Baby Killer* reached a combined print run of 20,000 copies in three English editions.

In the years following, many countries imposed regulations on the promotion of baby milks and positive programmes to encourage breast feeding were launched. Several public interest groups translated *The Baby Killer*. One such translation (by the Swiss based group, *Arbeitsgruppe Dritte Welt Bern*) sparked off a major wave of world publicity, for it changed the introduction and the title. Instead of calling it *The Baby Killer*, the title became *Nestlé Toetet Kinder* (Nestlé Kills Babies). The emphasis of the report was changed from a general view of the baby milk industry to one that specifically centred on Swiss-based Nestlé.

Nestlé responded quickly. In July 1974 it filed a libel suit against the Berne group. The case opened in November 1975, two days after the official launching of the International Council of Infant Food Industries (ICIFI), which had announced its intention to publish a code of ethics. Two days after the end of the first hearing, the ICIFI code was published. The 13 members of the Berne group were eventually found guilty of libel (the charge that the company killed infants could not be proved) and fined 300 Swiss francs each.

In July 1977 the US-based Infant Formula Action Coalition (INFACT) called for a boycott of Nestlé products until the company stopped all promotion of infant foods. In November 1978 the US National Council of Churches joined the boycott.

The activities of US-based action groups, plus the continued concern of health professionals, prompted the US Senate Subcommittee on Health and Scientific Research to hold a one day hearing in May 1978 to examine the advertising, promotion and use of infant formulas in developing nations. One outcome of this hearing was an approach by the Senate Committee's chairman, Edward Kennedy, to WHO to convene a meeting on the subject. WHO agreed and, together with UNICEF, called a meeting for October 1979 in Geneva to look at infant and young child feeding (Chetley, 1979).

This UNICEF/WHO meeting was unique in that it was the first international forum at which non-governmental organizations, including some of the most outspoken critics of the industry, were allowed to participate as full delegates. It was after this meeting that IBFAN, an international coalition of NGOs involved in this area, was formed. Its effective lobbying led to the adoption of the breast feeding code by the WHA in 1981.

Calling for a Code on Pharmaceutical Marketing

During the 1981 WHA some 50 NGOs concerned about the rational use of drugs came together in Geneva to form the HAI. Its goals were 'to further the safe, rational and economic use of pharmaceuticals world-wide, to promote the full implementation of WHO's Action Programme on Essential Drugs and to look for non-drug solutions to the problems created by impure water and poor sanitation and nutrition.' In anticipation of WHO introducing a code on pharmaceuticals and in response to the growing organizational strength of the consumer groups, in March 1981 IFPMA had taken the strategic decision to launch its own marketing code. In March 1982 it issued a supplementary statement which stressed the industry's commitment to observe and monitor this code and laid down procedures for dealing with any breaches of it. The code, which HAI (1982) criticized for being 'too general to be of any use', had a major impact on WHO's future activities vis-à-vis the private sector.

During the 35th WHA in 1982, delegates discussed the APED strategy and passed a strongly worded resolution urging WHO to implement it 'in its entirety'. In an unexpected development, the USA cooperated with Algeria, Switzerland, The Netherlands and the Nordic countries in drafting the motion which was unanimously adopted. HAI welcomed the resolution, while IFPMA deplored the fact that it did not mention its offer to cooperate with WHO (HAI, 1982). In a statement, the president of IFPMA stressed that the industry's offers in support of DAP should be seen as 'preparedness' to negotiate on 'non-commercial' prices for drugs for public health programmes in developing countries.

The new resolution followed discussions at the WHA during which The Netherlands made a forceful statement in support of international controls over pharmaceutical marketing. Its approach was endorsed by countries across the political spectrum. Chile, Cuba, Romania, Sudan, Ghana and Samoa all stressed the importance of WHO controls, which would enable developing countries to defend themselves against double standards in marketing and high drugs prices.

At the 1982 WHA, besides distributing a pamphlet criticizing the use of the anti-diarrhoeal drug, Lomotil, in developing countries, HAI also distributed a leaflet entitled *Not to be Taken, at Least not to be Taken Seriously* (HAI, 1982a), which was a detailed criticism of IFPMAs code and its supplement. HAI argued that the provisions in the code and the procedures for interpreting, monitoring and enforcing it were consistently and transparently inadequate, specifically commenting (HAI, 1982a: 13) that:

> The IFPMA says that many of the 'major associations' have already set up procedures for monitoring complaints. However, these major associations are almost exclusively based in the industrialized countries, when the need for effective regulation is in the third world. The procedure which IFPMA itself will use to deal with complaints is not explained. The reference to 'major sanctions of adverse publicity' is not at all convincing.

HAI concluded:

> In the absence of any convincing demonstration of the industry's commitment to regulate its own affairs, HAI's firm position will be to press hard for the introduction of a proper code of practice through WHO, UNCTAD and/or other appropriate part of the United Nations system.

Controversy continued at the 36th WHA the following year, when only the budgetary aspects of DAP were on the agenda. HAI representatives sought to remind delegates of the importance of essential drugs policy by distributing copies of new publications on pharmaceuticals and world health, notably the comprehensive analysis written by Diana Melrose of OXFAM and a draft international code on pharmaceuticals. The effect of the IFPMA code published earlier was already evident. For example, one of the Dutch delegates suggested that the *voluntary, self-disciplining approach* was to be preferred to the long and arduous process of international regulatory action. He stated that consideration should first be given to strengthening the IFPMA code, primarily through improving its enforcement structure. He then requested from the IFPMA representative information about the current state of compliance to the code by its member organizations and about ways in which governments could draw the attention of the industry to possible deviations from it (WHA, 1983). This statement was a step back from the previous year, when the Dutch delegation had argued in favour of WHO imposing controls over the marketing of drugs in the third world.

In reply to the request for information about the current status of compliance to the IFPMA code, its representative, Michael Peretz, noted that IFPMA itself so far had only received three complaints relating to 22 products. Two of these had been dealt with under the agreed procedure and were found to have nothing to do with marketing practices; the third involving one product was still under investigation. He reported that IFPMA had also carried out a careful audit of its member associations, noting that 'this audit has confirmed the commitment of individual companies to support and adhere to our code. In summary, the audit has demonstrated that there have been remarkably few substantiated cases of breaches of the code brought to either our attention or to that of our member associations' (Peretz, 1983). Peretz used the opportunity to stress IFPMA's support of the essential drugs concept in the form of:

> Supplying 150 substances included in the WHO Model List of Essential Drugs, plus another 100 not on the list, at favourable prices; offers of 15 companies to send experts to individual developing countries to help them with their logistics; setting up of pilot projects in Burundi (Swiss companies), Somalia (Italian companies) and The Gambia (US companies), with IFPMA playing an intermediary role making sure that the governments were put in contact with the appropriate companies; offering of training courses on quality control.

Meanwhile DAP had started to step up its support for essential drugs programmes in developing countries, initially focusing on Kenya and Tanzania where essential drugs policies were being implemented without formal cooperation from the industry. Generic drugs were being bought through drug tenders. It became clear that in response to such international tenders even major internationally operating companies were willing to provide essential drugs at remarkably low prices.

Heightened Politicization: The Industry on the Defensive

The period 1984-6 was crucial for DAP, both because of the rapid development of the scope of WHO's work in the field of pharmaceuticals and because of the heightened controversy surrounding the WHAs of 1984 and 1986 and the expert meeting on the rational use of drugs in Nairobi in 1985.

During the 1984 Executive Board (EB) meeting it was clear that the industry was on the defensive and fearful that WHO would take steps to develop a code on the marketing of pharmaceuticals. IFPMA was confronted with a DAP progress report which mentioned the European

Parliament's recommendation to develop a pharmaceutical marketing code, but only referred to IFPMA's role in passing. It also demonstrated the dramatic effects of efficient tendering on the prices of essential drugs and proposed adopting the 'idea' of essential drugs in a large number of developing countries. The report also specifically endorsed Bangladesh's new drugs policy.

The IFPMA representative, Peretz, tried without success to talk-up the extent of the industry's collaboration and the importance of its code. Peretz was supported by the US representative, Neil Boyer, who was very unhappy about the report. He complained that WHO officials had been monitoring adherence to the IFPMA code by sending in complaints to IFPMA headquarters. He asked WHO not to embark on monitoring the code of a private sector organization and suggested that 'it is not a good idea to bite the hand that feeds you a nutritious meal' (Guest, 1984). This rather cryptic remark was supposed to warn WHO of the possible actions not only the industry might take but also, perhaps, the major contributors to WHO's budget.

At the 1984 WHA, the delegates, led by The Netherlands and the Nordic countries, with support from HAI and its partner the International Organization of Consumer Unions (IOCU), asked the director-general to organize a meeting to which representatives of governments, national regulatory agencies, the pharmaceutical industry, consumer groups, NGOs and the medical profession would be invited to discuss the rational use of drugs. These representatives were subsequently referred to as the Group of Interested Parties.

HAI had spent many months planning and raising funds for its activities at the 1984 WHA. The network's overall strategy was to 'inject a short, sharp dose of reality' about drugs market conditions into the diplomatic niceties of the WHA proceedings. Various strategies used included a video called *Hard to Swallow*, a conference newspaper called *Health Now*, an exhibition and intensive lobbying of conference delegates by a team of lobbyists from 13 countries, who discussed the drugs issue with individual delegates and supplied them with specially prepared documentation. When the resolution calling for an expert meeting on rational drugs use was passed, a HAI spokeswoman commented: 'At last we are beginning to see action. There is now a consensus that uncontrolled drug markets cannot meet urgent health needs. HAI is delighted that some major drug producing countries today put consumer needs before purely commercial interests by voting for the resolution.' HAI's tactics had been effective.

The consequent WHO conference of experts on the rational use of drugs was held in Nairobi in November 1985. In an attempt to prevent controversies and lobbying *before* the actual conference took place, the WHO Secretariat kept the list of participants secret. The 92 participants, drawn from governments, national drugs regulatory authorities, the pharmaceutical industry, consumer and patient groups, health care providers, academics and representatives from other UN agencies and from NGOs, were asked by the

WHO Secretariat not to divulge the contents of the ten background papers in advance of the conference. These papers, which had been prepared by consultants, had been 'modified' by the WHO Secretariat. The paper on the distribution and use of pharmaceuticals in developing countries was, according to its authors, 'skilfully augmented, rewritten and presented to participants in a format more compatible with WHO's need for an objective context rather than a provocative one', which led the authors to publish the paper elsewhere in its original form (Fabricant and Hirschorn, 1987). An edition of WHO's *Essential Drugs Monitor*, due out before the conference and planning to give extensive coverage of the issues to be discussed, was scrapped. The meeting itself was intended to be conducted in much the same manner as a WHA, with participants given an average of ten minutes each to speak on the various themes the Secretariat had placed on the agenda (Chetley, 1985; SCRIP, 1985: 17).

The industry was still anxious about the possibility that the Nairobi meeting would provide the basis for a code on marketing pharmaceuticals, in the same way as the meeting on infant feeding in 1979 had helped launch the WHO infant formula code two years later (IOMS, 1985). HAI, however, had recognized the futility of arguing for a code and had already changed its strategy for the conference. An indication of this change in policy is found in the leading HAI activist Charles Medawar's presentation at a seminar called Another Development in Pharmaceuticals, organized by the Dag Hammarskjöld Foundation in Sweden in June 1985 prior to the Nairobi meeting. He (Medawar, 1985) notes that:

> Effective regulation implies the need for (a) clearly defined objectives and clear policies and standards; (b) machinery for monitoring and obtaining feedback on practice observed; (c) the ability to explain and justify enforcement decisions taken as a result; and (d) the power to impose sanctions. Clearly, WHO is in no position to enforce standards along these lines. Equally, it has no wish for confrontation, either with the richer member governments, or with the industry.... It is therefore unrealistic to expect WHO to become involved in formal, full-scale international regulation.

Instead, Medawar called on WHO to outline 'minimum standards relating to the supply and use of drugs'. These could then be applied to all countries. In line with this analysis HAI's strategy shifted from the concept of a code to one of more general standards, but more importantly it was working towards limiting the number of drugs on the market, arguing that there is no point in trying to control the supply and use of thousands of drugs that are not essential in the first place. The shift also meant that HAI's attention would be focused more on national level implementation of essential drugs policies and less on the adoption of supranational regulations.

Was HAI right, given the success of the breast milk substitutes code, to assume that a pharmaceuticals code would be an unrealistic goal? Two points need to be considered. First, as was clear from reports on the health related industry by the International Organization Monitoring Services (IOMS), a New York based business consultancy financed by subscriptions from multinationals and other industrial clients, IFPMA had learnt from the infant formula experience. The IOMS had repeatedly confronted the pharmaceutical industry with developments in the infant formula field and IFPMA had effectively pre-empted the emergence of a WHO code by developing its own, which it claimed to be monitoring. The second point is that the infant formula code was not much more than a list of 'minimum standards' that needed to be legislated at the national level. Although under Articles 21 and 22 of its constitution WHO has a mandate to set and enforce regulations, which are binding for all member countries without the need for ratification, acceptance or approval by each member, the 1981 EB meeting decided that the code would have the status of a 'recommendation'. The EB argued that a recommendation's moral force might be more effective than the legal pressure of a regulation; it would preserve the national sovereignty of member countries in applying the code at the national level, rather than applying it as an international obligation. It would take into account differences in national constitutional and legal systems. It might better gain the unanimous approval of all members and it would be easier to monitor and revise (Leonard, 1986).

The Nairobi Conference: 1985

In an introductory statement at the first meeting of the Nairobi conference, the director-general reminded participants that they were there as experts and not as representatives of any of the interested parties. He went on to say that the aim of the conference was to ensure that people, particularly in developing countries, had access to the drugs they needed; it was not intended to be an international battleground for the pharmaceutical industry and consumers to vent their interests. (For a detailed report of the Nairobi conference, see WHO, 1985.)

During the conference there were over 200 interventions on the following discussion items: national drugs policies, drugs marketing, national essential drugs programmes, research, the WHO certification scheme, quality control, and education and training. The need to restrict the number of drugs on the market to the essential ones, thereby stopping the manufacture or import of those that do not really help patients, was a central theme of the discussions. Some of the participants saw this rationalization of the pharmaceuticals market as a prerequisite to the successful implementation of other components of a national drugs policy, such as quality control or providing information about the drugs. Others, however, opposed this view on the grounds that drugs are already restricted in that no individual prescribers or hospitals use more than the limited number they themselves have selected and that limiting the number of drugs deprives patients of the best possible treatment and is a major disincentive to pharmaceutical research.

The meeting agreed that a national drugs policy should ensure that drugs of acceptable quality, safety and efficacy are available at affordable costs to all who need them (wherever and whenever they need them) to combat the diseases prevalent in the country in question and to improve or maintain the health of its inhabitants. It was emphasized that such a policy needs *political will* on the part of governments. It was felt that at the international level WHO should disseminate guidelines on national drugs policies. These were eventually published in 1988.

The meeting recognized that a rational use of drugs implied that the people most intimately concerned, i.e. the prescribers and consumers, must receive the information they needed to use drugs rationally. Much of the discussion centred around how information on drugs could be made more objective and more accessible. It was pointed out that in many countries the industry was the main source of information and that this was inevitably biased because it was geared towards selling the products. It was suggested that governments and professional organizations should make better use of their opportunities to disseminate complete and unbiased information on drugs.

With regard to information to consumers, it was said that this should be presented clearly and simply in the inserts in drugs packages, as well as in the instructions given to consumers. Some saw the role of the mass media as very important in reaching consumers. Others felt that the mass media tended to distort and sensationalize the issues. A suggestion was made that information and learning materials should be included in the UNICEF drugs kits. Many felt that WHO should increase the number of expert meetings, workshops and seminars so that it would be in a better position to produce guidelines on the many aspects of providing information for and teaching about the rational use of drugs, but these guidelines never materialized.

The conference agreed that governments were responsible for regulating marketing, which was seen as the whole range of activities between the manufacture and consumption of drugs. Some participants stressed that the pharmaceutical industry's marketing practices, particularly in promotion, all too often led to a demand for inessential drugs that did not meet health needs. Critics regarded sales representatives as aggressive promoters and felt that their use of free samples was particularly undesirable in that some prescribers sold them for personal gain. Others felt that they gave prescribers valuable counselling and useful first hand information on new drugs in return for feedback on side effects and adverse reactions. Doubts were also expressed about the use of the mass media to advertise drugs. It was said that such advertising encouraged the public to indulge in self-medication.

The participants believed there should be ethical criteria for advertising drugs. These were published by WHO in 1988. The major responsibility for ensuring that ethical criteria were observed, it was held, lay with the industry. It was suggested that the IFPMA code had not been effective in this regard. Other participants, however, defended the code.

There was a sharp clash of views between the industry and some delegates over the 'universality' of rationalizing the drugs sector. On the one hand was the argument that the private sector had an important role to play in delivering essential drugs and must, therefore, be controlled in the interests of public health; on the other hand, however, representatives of the industry argued that rationalization should be confined to the public sector. There was also disagreement over the extent to which the number of drugs should be reduced and by what criteria. Some experts argued strongly in favour of a Norwegian style 'needs clause'. In Norway drugs policy stipulates that, apart from being safe, any new drug has to be shown to be *more* effective than those already on the market and that there should be a clearcut need for any new product. Experts representing the industry and governments of major drugs producing nations saw the 'needs clause' approach as potentially detrimental to the research and development of new drugs. (WHO's official report of the meeting makes no mention of the clash of views in Nairobi, though *Health Now*, the newspaper the consumer organizations distributed at the 1986 WHA, does. See Chetley, 1986.)

Fringe Conflicts

Despite WHO's efforts to avoid controversy, there were some disputes in the 'corridors' of the Nairobi meeting. The US-based Heritage Foundation antagonized the WHO Secretariat by slipping its own material (Brooks, 1985) into WHO's information pack for journalists. As a conservative think tank, the Heritage Foundation is believed to have the ear of the Republican administration and the support of large segments of US industry. It often acts as a surrogate spokesperson for conservative industrial interests (IOMS, 1986). The Heritage Foundation material urged experts to oppose 'medical need' as a criteria for evaluating drugs. Dr Mahler called the incident a 'highly undesirable practice' and said that he would report the matter to the local authorities. There was also a dispute about *The Pill Jungle*, a film co-produced by WHO and paid for with DAP funds. The industry's representatives opined that the film was biased, with a distinct consumer group imprint. WHO cancelled screening and, at a press conference, Dr Mahler explained that the film 'was disturbing a very important group of experts' and that it was his duty to 'try to recreate serenity'. (For accounts of these controversies see Chetley, 1990.)

In summing up the conference, Mahler pointed out that the experts had invited WHO to take a leadership role without becoming 'a supranational manipulator of governments'. He suggested that WHO establish expert committees to produce guidelines on ethical advertising and on developing national drugs policies. He emphasized that at no time during the meeting had a case been made for developing an international code (SCRIP, 1985a; WHO, 1985).

The conference had neither accepted the code nor endorsed the 'medical need' criterion. WHO had not assumed the role of a supranational regulatory agency and the conference had not been used as a major propaganda platform for the industry's critics. Nevertheless, the industry's representatives felt that their critics had gained legitimacy from the conference. They had participated as experts and, as such, had substantially influenced the content of the discussions and the outcome of the conference. There was good reason to fear their continued participation in the expert committees, at which guidelines for advertising and national drugs policies would be developed. As the president of the US Pharmaceutical Manufacturers Association (PMA) put it in a memo to its member companies: 'The proposal of the director-general to ask the 1986 WHA to set up a series of "committees of experts" will provide the international activists with a continuing series of "mini-Nairobi's" to get press attention and to chip away at the firm resolve of WHO not to become an international regulatory body.'

The industry's continued fear of a code was also reflected by the IOMS (1985): 'It is extremely likely that a resolution will be proposed at the May 1986 WHA which will use the Nairobi conference results as the excuse to pursue a pharmaceutical code. IOMS sources strongly suggest that such a resolution is already being conceptualized by the Nordic bloc governments in cooperation with HAI members.' Despite these fears, IFPMA issued a press statement after the conference in which it 'welcomed the low-key discussion of the many issues involved' and supported 'Dr Mahler's firm conclusions that the WHO cannot perform as a supranational regulatory body' (IFPMA, 1985).

The Revised Drugs Strategy

The 1986 WHA following the Nairobi conference endorsed the revised drugs strategy, a proposal for action prepared by the Secretariat and based on the outcome of the Nairobi conference. This strategy aimed to make the use of drugs more rational throughout the world. It required WHO to secure the cooperation of a number of 'concerned parties', including governments, the pharmaceutical industry, health care personnel, NGOs, consumer and patient groups and the public, and called on these concerned parties to take responsibility for implementing the strategy. It also mentioned that it was WHO's responsibility, through the convening of expert meetings, to draw up the ethical criteria for drugs promotion and to set guidelines for developing national drugs policies.

The revised drugs strategy was unanimously accepted. Neither the industry nor the consumer activists could oppose it, for they had supported its underlying principles by accepting the director-general, Mahler's, summing up at the end of the Nairobi conference. He had made a plea to delegates to retain the cooperative 'spirit of Nairobi' throughout the debate.

Despite overall support for the revised drugs strategy, the industry and consumer groups lobbied the 1986 WHA more intensely than ever. Prepared for the worst, IFPMA had set up a press centre and exhibition and was issuing a considerable amount of material about the pharmaceutical industry's contribution to the research and development of new drugs and to their supply and distribution in the third world. At the WHA, the IFPMA president declared (SCRIP, 1986): 'We do not accept any interpretation of the revised drugs strategy which would inhibit the development of new medicines by implying that subjective criteria [such as the need clause] should be introduced into the registration process. Nor do we accept that a drastic reduction in the number of permitted drugs represents a practical path of progress'. With regard to advertising and promotion he continued:

> [The IFPMA] fully accepts the importance of universal ethical standards although we seriously question whether the inclusion of this subject among the projects in the revised drugs strategy will do much to improve drugs supply and use in the developing countries.... I would remind delegates that our code requires neither national regulation nor government administrative or financial resources for its operation.

HAI, in turn, launched a 'problem drugs pack' of major pharmaceutical drugs categories throughout the world (HAI, 1985), in which it was argued that the industry's claims that marketing problems were limited to a 'few errant drugs, unethically promoted by one or two rogue elephants in industry', were wrong. It showed that the problems were actually 'an inevitable result of the way in which the pharmaceutical market is structured and operates' (HAI, 1985; IOMS, 1986a; SCRIP, 1986). In addition, HAI published its newspaper, *Health Now*, as it had done during the 1984 WHA.

The heightened politicization during the 1986 WHA was also caused by the more active role of the US government in lobbying other governments to oppose the possibility of WHO becoming involved in regulating the industry's operations in developing countries. This was reflected in an intervention by the US delegate to WHO during the debate on the marketing code for breast milk substitutes. In his speech, attached to the IOMS (1986a) report, he stated that:

> I think that most delegations know that the United States was the only country to vote against the adoption of the breast milk substitutes marketing code in 1981. Before then and ever since, it has been our strong position that the World Health Organization should not be involved in efforts to regulate or control the commercial practices of private industry, even when the products may relate to concerns about health.

US delegates lobbied for a 'resolution for reaffirmation'. Drafted by a US member of the former Commission on UNESCO, the resolution called for reaffirmation of basic WHO objectives. It decried the 'alarming prospects of politicizing health' and urged concentration on 'primary standards of health care' rather than 'attempts to regulate commercial products' (Reaffirmation Group, 1986). This resolution was not adopted.

The US delegation seemed to have been led to its position by a Heritage Foundation report entitled 'For the World Health Organization, the Moment of Truth' (Heritage Foundation, 1986). The basic premise of this report was that WHO was becoming increasingly politicized and, as UNESCO did before, would soon face a 'moment of truth' when it must either reform or lose the support of the US. The report cited WHO developments on a whole variety of issues, including the Palestinian problem, infant food regulation and regulation of the pharmaceutical industry, as well as the Health for All strategy, which was seen as a 'blueprint that tilts far against private sector health care systems in favour of state run systems which, experience painfully teaches, fail to deliver medicines or care'. Among others things, it recommended (Heritage Foundation, 1986: 11) that the US should 'oppose any attempts by WHO to regulate advertising by private companies; protest [against] over-zealous, inappropriate activism by WHO employees; and implement fully the legislatively mandated budgetary cuts to force WHO to spend its reduced funds on health rather than politics.'

US pressure did not seem to have the desired impact. In its assessment of the 1986 WHA, the IOMS (1986: 1) states:

> This WHA demonstrated four main lessons for companies: (a) WHO is now firmly down the path of regulating businesses which affect human health; (b) WHO 'soft' regulation [i.e. the proposed ethical criteria on promotion and the guidelines for national drugs policies] gradually will take on a hard character as long as the critics maintain their pressure; (c) the IOCU and its allies are here to stay, demonstrating increasing sophistication and constantly reminding companies that they are capable of major surprises hurting the industry interests; (d) the activists are carving out an increased role for themselves as the eyes, ears and muscle of WHO as WHO finds itself unable to implement its own programmes the way it would like to due to budgetary constraints.

On the limited impact of US lobbying, the report (IOMS 1986: 13) comments that: 'The US government is opposing this transformation of WHO. But it finds defence of industry interests difficult because those very industries are heavily regulated within the US for the same reasons now being used by advocates of international regulations at the World Health Assemblies.' In 1986 the US failed to pay its contribution to WHO. Though no formal reason was given, the non-payment was generally believed to be related to WHO's activities in the drugs field.

More Emphasis on National-level Implementation: 1986-90

In the years following the adoption of the revised drugs strategy, no 'hard' regulations were adopted. In line with its approach at the Nairobi conference, WHO tried to ensure that the 'expert meetings' were serene forums of discussion on the issues under consideration. Experts were invited in their personal capacity rather than as representatives of 'concerned parties' and no resolutions were to be adopted by the meetings. By 1988, when the 41st WHA was due to discuss the progress of the revised drugs strategy, three of the six planned expert meetings had been held, one on developing guidelines for national drugs policies, one on setting out the ethical criteria for promoting drugs and an additional one on the WHO certification scheme. Of the three remaining ones, the absence of an expert meeting on patient and prescribing information and education was most apparent. It was this subject that had been seen to require a follow-up conference during the Nairobi meeting on the rational use of drugs.

The results of the expert meetings that did take place testified to the heavy political constraints under which WHO operates. For example, the guidelines for establishing national drugs policies failed to signify the importance of regulating the private sector or of significantly reducing the number of drugs on the market. As Ernst Lauridsen, head of DAP commented, 'if governments have the political will to introduce essential drugs policies, then this paper will give them a useful framework, if they haven't got that political will then no paper will help.' A similarly weak attempt to set standards of industrial practice emerged from the meeting on ethical criteria for promoting drugs. In an information brief on the 41st WHA, HAI commented:

> In an attempt to ensure that guidelines are produced which stand a chance of surviving the various committees, the EB and the WHA, a document has been drawn up which is considerably weaker than many industry voluntary codes and no better than the IFPMA code. The guidelines fail to set any real standards with regard to samples, symposia, qualities of promotional material, free gifts, etc. Advertisements without product information are considered permissible if they can be deemed 'reminder advertisements'.

The election at the 1988 EB meeting of Dr Nakajima, regional director of WPRO, as the new director-general of WHO introduced a new element into WHO politics, with rather depressing implications for DAP. This pessimism set the atmosphere for the 1988 WHA debate on drugs.

The WHO Secretariat presented the delegates with a report on ethical criteria for promoting drugs. Though providing a commentary on these criteria, HAI did not lobby against the proposed resolution endorsing the guidelines the EB had presented to the WHA. This surprised the pharmaceutical industry which, still fearing that some delegates in consultation with HAI would be calling for a more stringent code, had decided to support the resolution. Instead, HAI strengthened its links with delegates of third world countries, thereby reflecting its shift in focus away from international regulations towards national level implementation of essential drugs policies.

Thus, the 1988 WHA was far less politicized than the 1986 one had been. While in the early 1980s HAI had constantly been trying to persuade WHO to broaden the scope of the essential drugs concept to include regulation of the private sector, to limit the number of drugs on the market and to implement the policies in both developing and industrialized nations, it now appeared to be defending DAP and the revised drugs strategy and calling on delegates to push for its continued implementation. It was clear that the US and IFPMA were looking forward to better times.

In a report prepared for the 43rd annual WHA in 1990, Dr Nakajima told the delegates that IFPMA had adopted a memorandum of intent, which confirmed the willingness of the international pharmaceutical industry 'to

62 *Consumers versus Producers*

cooperate with WHO to improve access to health care for populations in need, particularly in the developing world'. In this memorandum (IFPMA, 1990) the primary contribution of the pharmaceutical industry to world health is declared to be 'through research into new medicines' and 'through the development, production and supply of new, improved and established products.' In addition, it states that 'the industry readily accepts a role which extends beyond its normal commercial activities, as a partner with others, to provide assistance in countries and regions where adequate health care is seriously lacking.'

At the 1990 WHA, HAI lobbied the delegates to support the continued implementation of the revised drugs strategy. HAI supported a resolution (WHO, 1990) drafted by the Dutch delegation and adopted by the WHA, in which the director-general was requested 'to strengthen his support for the promotion of the essential drugs concept as part of the revised drugs strategy' and 'to report to the Executive Board and the 45th World Health Assembly on the use of the ethical criteria for drugs promotion.'

In Conclusion

From the above it is clear that the pharmaceutical industry and US representatives at the WHAs put pressure on WHO to confine essential drugs policies to the public sector in poor countries. Any attempts by WHO to regulate, monitor or make recommendations about the private sector activities of transnational pharmaceutical companies were strongly resisted. In this debate the US consistently opposed state intervention in health care in general (opining that privatized health care is more cost effective) and thus undermined WHO's Health for All strategy. The US prefers to regard WHO as a technical support agency and disapproves of it advocating that the state intervene in and control the health care market. This pressure effectively prevented WHO from developing either a code or strong guidelines on the marketing, distribution and use of pharmaceuticals in developing countries. Whereas the previous leadership kept DAP alive and on the move, in recent years the current leadership appears to have curtailed the action programme and limited the role of WHO to that of providing technical support.

Consumer groups cooperating with HAI played a significant part in helping to formulate WHO's policy. They lobbied to expand the essential drugs concept to include setting standards for the pharmaceutical industry's private sector activities and adopting a revised drugs strategy, which laid the basis for coordinated international action in the field of essential drugs. They constantly repeated that any rationalization of pharmaceutical distribution and use should include reducing the number of drugs on the market and that the criteria for this should be safety, efficacy, cost and medical need. They called for universal acceptance of the essential drugs concept. At the WHA they mainly cooperated with third world, Nordic and Dutch government delegations, which resulted in the drafting and adoption of a number of resolutions in support of DAP and the revised drugs strategy. It is remarkable that a resolution calling for the continued implementation of the revised drugs strategy and the adoption of ethical criteria was accepted at the 1990 WHA. However, more importantly perhaps, the consumer groups reached government representatives, national policy-makers and, increasingly, the public in developed and developing countries. They heightened their awareness of the issues involved and called on their support for comprehensive national essential drugs policies, covering both private and public sectors. This advocacy role had a practical impact on the development of a critical mass of people working to promote essential drugs policies both in developing and developed countries.

The most decisive role in this whole controversy was probably played by the WHO leadership, especially during the preparation and conduct of the Nairobi meeting. Bringing together as experts people with often opposing positions and interests and getting them to agree on the general principles for the revised drugs strategy, not only deflated antagonism but also provided an important basis for DAP's work for years to come.

References

Brooks, R.A. (1985) 'Saving the World Health Organization from a poison pill'. *The Heritage Foundation Backgrounder*, 471, 19 November, Washington

Chetley, A (1979) *The baby killer scandal*, London: War on Want

————— (1985) 'Veil of secrecy over international drugs meeting'. *Gemini News Service*, London (GH 37), 8 November

————— (1986) 'Will the spirit of Nairobi prevail in Geneva'. *Health Now*, 2, 5 May

————— (1990) *The global pharmaceutical industry: A health industry or a healthy business.* London: Zed Books

Fabricant, S.J. and N. Hirschorn (1987) 'Deranged distribution, perverse prescription and unprotected use: The irrationality of pharmaceuticals in the developing world'. *Health Policy and Planning*, 2 (3), 204-13

Guest, I. (1984) *The Guardian*, 21 January, London

HAI (1982) *HAI News*, June

————— (1982a) *Not to be taken, at least not to be taken seriously.* Geneva: HAI

————— (1985) *Problem drugs pack.* The Hague: HAI

Heritage Foundation (1986) 'For the World Health Organization, the moment of truth: A United Nations assessment project'. *Heritage Foundation Backgrounder*, 30 April, Washington

IFPMA (1985) 'IFPMA preliminary view on rational use of drugs conference', IFPMA press release, 29 November, Zurich

————— (1990) *Memorandum of intent on cooperation between WHO and IFPMA on pharmaceutical industry projects intended to improve health care especially in the third world*, Zurich: IFPMA

IOMS (1985) *World Health Organization: Results of the Nairobi conference on the rational use of drugs.* New York: IOMS
————— (1986) *World Health Organization: Heritage Foundation report on the politicization of WHO.* New York: IOMS
————— (1986a) *Consumer protection: WHA: Results of the 1986 WHA.* New York: IOMS
Jelliffe, D. (1971) 'Commerciogenic malnutrition?' *Food Tech,* 25, 55
Leonard, S. (1986) 'International health and transnational business: Conflict or cooperation? *Review Internationale des Sciences Administratives,* 49 (3), 259-68
Medawar, C. (1985) 'International regulation of the supply and use of pharmaceuticals'. *Development Dialogue,* 2, 29
Peretz, Michael (1983) 'IFPMA's presentation to Committee A, 36th WHA'
Reaffirmation Group (1986) *Will there be a reaffirmation of WHO's basic principles?* Published privately by the Reaffirmation Group at the 39th WHA, Geneva
Reich, M. (1987) 'Essential drugs: Economics and politics in international health'. *Health Policy,* 8, 39-57
SCRIP (1985) *100 Delegates for Nairobi meeting.* 1047, 30 October, 7
————— (1985a) *Mahler sums up at Nairobi.* 1059, 20
————— (1986) *WHA endorses WHO's revised drug strategy.* 1105, 17
WHA (1983) *Summary proceedings.* Geneva: WHO
WHO (1985) 'Rational use of drugs: Cooperation prevails at WHO conference in "spirit of Nairobi"'. Press release, WHO/32, Geneva
————— (1990) 'Action Programme on Essential Drugs'. 43rd WHA, agenda item no. 23

4

Action at Country Level: The International and National Influences

Najmi Kanji

This chapter begins by describing the components of a rational pharmaceutical policy as defined by WHO. It goes on to analyse why and how national pharmaceutical policies in different countries are influenced by powerful outside actors. Finally, it looks at the dynamics and the various national interests within developing countries that determine the development, or not, of rational drugs policies.

In 1977, WHO's newly established Drug Policies and Management (DPM) unit convened an expert committee to produce a model essential drugs list. The official publication of this list in the same year with the WHO imprimatur was a critical tool for furthering a new approach to drugs policy (WHO, 1977). The introductory section to this document clearly outlined the conceptual and technical bases for the essential drugs concept and specified the complementary policy, legislative, logistic and educational actions necessary to ensure the regular supply and rational use of drugs. The establishment of the administrative unit for the Action Programme on Essential Drugs, with the acronym DAP (Drugs Action Programme) in 1981, led to the crystallization of the essential drugs concept into components which WHO identified as necessary for a rational pharmaceutical policy (WHO, 1988). The major components and the rationale behind them are shown below.

Components of a Rational Drugs Policy

Essential drugs lists: Countries identify a limited number of drugs that reflect the pathology and therefore the priority needs of the population. These lists should be made up of generic drugs proven to be therapeutically effective, acceptably safe and of lowest cost.

Legislation, registration and quality assurance: National pharmaceutical policies require legislation that promotes rationality. Drug regulatory authorities with adequate staff and powers are necessary to ensure that only drugs within the list are registered and authorized to circulate within the country. Appropriate legislation and strong regulatory agencies, together with the ability to carry out quality control tests on imported or locally produced drugs, ensure a degree of quality assurance for the drugs used within a particular country.

Procurement and distribution: To obtain the best terms in relation to costs and delivery times, national drugs procurement should be centralized and drugs should be bought by generic names through international tenders. The distribution of these drugs should be planned so as to be regular and to reflect the greater needs at primary level services. Distribution should also correspond to assessments of the quantities required at the various levels of health care.

Local production: The development of local production capabilities, where feasible, should help to reduce the dependence of developing countries on industrialized countries for their drugs needs and also increase the rate of technology transfer from the industrialized to the developing nations.

Education and training: Benefits derived from rationalizing the selection, procurement and distribution of drugs are greatly diminished if health staff do not have the necessary knowledge and skills to use the drugs correctly. Thus the essential drugs concept, as well as the technical information about the drugs, should be known by and be readily available to all health staff authorized to use drugs. The training of new staff should reflect these aspects.

Information for the public: The public should be informed not only about the importance of complying with the instructions given by the prescriber, but also about the potential hazards associated with exaggerated auto-medication. The public should also be made aware of the limited role drugs can play in improving their health.

Research: For monitoring and evaluating the efficacy and safety of the drugs utilized, the role of traditional medicines and the socio-economic and socio-cultural aspects of drugs use, research is an important tool and contributes to the development of rational pharmaceutical policies.

The implementation of rational drugs policies at national level has, however, raised complex issues which have not easily been resolved. These include:

The Universality of the Essential Drugs Concept

Though resolutions in support of the concept have been passed at various World Health Assemblies (WHAs), the focus of WHO's activity has been on the developing world. Though justifiable on the grounds that the need for rationalization has been greater in developing countries, to make essential drugs available to the majority of the population, this focus on the availability of drugs has led some to argue that the concept is valid and necessary for developing countries only, because essential drugs are available to all in developed countries. Others argue that the concept is just as applicable in developed countries because the problem there is more related to the abundance of inessential drugs.

Supply or Use

Supporters of radical change in the pharmaceutical environment argue that the supply (availability) of essential drugs is only part of the essential drugs concept. In their view the question of rational drugs use is a much more serious issue. They argue that the availability of essential drugs has a limited benefit if the drugs are not used correctly. Training and supervision of health professionals, the dissemination of objective information to professionals and the public, research into the efficacy and safety of drugs and the monitoring of their adverse effects are all vital to the promotion and implementation of essential drugs policies. Others feel that this is a difficult area and interferes with the clinician's freedom to prescribe and that the dissemination of cautionary information to the public can only be counter productive. In practice, the tendency has been to focus on the supply side, for this is relatively easier to implement, though the more comprehensive issue of use is now much more firmly on international and national agendas.

Public or Private Sector Issue

The debate here also touches on the supply or use question. If the major issue is *supply*, then it is argued that the private sector plays an important role in supplying drugs to the public, so the essential drugs concept is usually confined to rationalizing supply in the public sector. However, if the issue is rational drugs *use*, then many argue that the private sector is often guilty of promoting irrational drugs use and, therefore, must be included in an essential drugs policy. There is also an economic argument. The implementation of an essential drugs policy covering the private sector would potentially curtail profits. Given that restrictive legislation in the private sector is an issue that touches the core of a country's political and economic ideology, the debate on whether the essential drugs concept should apply equally to both the public and private sectors has been intense and highly charged.

Restrictions or Recommendations

Problems have also arisen in deciding whether or not the essential drugs lists should be mandatory. Proponents of the essential drugs concept argue that, unless drugs lists are restricted by law, there is little hope of achieving rationalization in drugs use, given the power of the pharmaceutical industry and the medical views regarding the need to maintain prescribing freedom. Opponents argue that legal restrictions dilute a doctor's right to prescribe what he or she considers necessary for a patient and deprive patients of choice when particular drugs do not suit them. In addition, they argue that restrictions are potentially confrontational and should therefore be avoided.

Another implementation issue is whether or not the essential drugs lists should apply only to primary level services, thus excluding higher levels of health care (hospitals) on the grounds that these are staffed by doctors who are well trained to use them and need a wide array of drugs for specific, relatively uncommon conditions. The question of applying essential drugs programmes in a vertical fashion, which further fragments already weakly integrated primary health care (PHC) programmes, has also generated much debate. Some of these issues are further discussed below.

Though some countries had already developed rational drugs policies in the late 1960s and early 1970s, the economic crisis of the late 1970s and early 1980s activated renewed discussions about the possibility of implementing rational drugs policies. Reduced health budgets and the limited availability of convertible currency created drugs shortages in most countries. The generally skewed allocation of resources in favour of urban hospitals meant that these shortages were most acute in the primary services in rural areas and the supply of drugs to this level became a major priority. At about the same time, WHO had begun to take the lead in advocating the essential drugs concept as a way of using limited funds in the most cost-effective and therapeutically beneficial way and promoted the implementation of essential drugs programmes (EDPs) as a first step in the development of national policies based upon the essential drugs concept.

The difference between a drugs programme and a rational drugs policy has not always been appreciated. The two terms have been used interchangeably in their conceptual and operational aspects. The blurring of this distinction enabled interested parties to promote or prevent the radical and comprehensive restructuring of national drugs supply systems. For WHO, there was a twofold rationale behind implementing EDPs: (a) The PHC approach could only work if drugs were made available to primary level services, thereby giving credibility to the preventive and promotional activities central to the approach. It was crucial to integrate EDPs into other health programmes being implemented at primary level. And (b), by implementing EDPs in geographically restricted areas, the supply and availability of essential drugs could be dramatically improved at an acceptably low cost. This would provide an incentive for governments to base their policies on the essential drugs concept.

For international and national interests that saw rational drugs policies as a threat to monetary profit and professional power, the EDPs were ends in themselves. They could solve the problem of drugs shortages at the level of the primary services catering for the rural poor and, therefore, there was no need to change the existing drugs supply system.

In formulating and implementing drugs policies and programmes, countries have been constrained by their own political and economic ideologies. The question is not whether or not to rationalize the system, but rather how much of the system to rationalize without upsetting the many vested interests. Thus, in some countries EDPs have developed into comprehensive national policies involving a total rationalization of the drugs system, while in others they have remained mainly supply programmes making essential drugs available to public sector primary level facilities.

The recent evaluation of DAP, which includes 13 country studies, provides information on the development of rational drugs policies in these countries. It shows how the essential drugs concept has been interpreted differently by each country to suit its own political and economic environment (LSHTM/KIT, 1989). In all 13 countries EDPs have been implemented with the support of donor funding and WHO technical assistance, but in only two of these has the programme developed into a comprehensive national drugs policy based on the essential drugs concept.

In the following section an illustration is provided of how international drugs companies, WHO, bilateral donors and UNICEF, all important actors in the drugs field, have influenced national policy development. The second part of this chapter then focuses on the national players influencing the development of policy.

International Drug Companies

'The primary motivation of multinationals is profit maximization. Essential drugs policies are need-oriented rather than profit-motivated and therefore a conflict of interest is evident from the outset' (War on Want, 1982). In 1986 the pharmaceutical industry's annual turnover was roughly US$100,000 million. During the recession of the late 1970s and early 1980s, two of the very few industries continuing to make large profits were the arms industry and the drugs industry. The pharmaceutical industry's often vehement opposition to the development of rational drugs policies is based on the fear of its profits being curtailed. The controversies at international level (documented in earlier chapters) have not, however, prevented the adoption of essential drugs policies within countries, though international drugs companies have often tried to obstruct governments in their efforts to rationalize their pharmaceutical environments.

The structure of the pharmaceutical industry in developing countries needs to be described to understand the converging and diverging views within the industry. In countries with non-existent or negligible pharmaceutical production, transnational companies promote their products through sales representatives. Such countries buy their drugs through international tenders, in which the local representatives of the transnational companies bid. Foreign currency is made available to both the public and private sectors by the government. Local entrepreneurs are either only peripherally involved in the bidding or function as agents for transnational companies. In some cases they may produce certain bulk preparations, such as ointments or syrups. There is little potential for conflict of interests between national and foreign entrepreneurs. Countries such as Mozambique, Burundi, Democratic Yemen and the Yemen Arab Republic (YAR) before amalgamation in 1991, fall into this group.

In countries where local production is significant, national producers or wholesalers compete with transnational companies. In such countries, local subsidiaries of transnational companies often produce some of their products locally under licence from the parent company. National producers are often involved in the production of bulk galenic preparations and increasingly in the manufacture of popular drugs with expired patents. In addition, the government may also be involved in the production of drugs, either through owning public manufacturing companies or through joint ventures with the private sector. A local producer manufacturing generic diazepam often finds himself competing against the transnational Hoffman-La Roche, selling and promoting Valium. Moreover, as transnationals are increasingly producing generics, the competition between national producers and transnationals can be quite fierce. Whereas both these groups may well oppose any policy that restricts the activities of the private sector, their views over protective measures for the promotion of local (national) industry may well differ. Both groups can be powerful actors in influencing policy. Kenya, Nigeria and Zimbabwe are examples of countries in which there is a significant local production of drugs.

The third group of developing countries includes those that produce up to 90 per cent of their drugs locally, with sophisticated manufacturing facilities. In these countries, the drugs market is likely to be large, with intense competition between local entrepreneurs and transnational manufacturers. Governments often introduce regulations that are contradictory. For example, some governments have offered special incentives to transnational companies (tax exemption, government subsidies, profit repatriation facilities) which are sources of resentment to the local manufacturers. They may also offer preferential treatment to local or public manufacturers by buying public sector drugs from them. This is often seen as unfair by the transnationals. Once again, both these groups are able to exert much influence on the policy process. The Philippines, Indonesia, India and Colombia fall into this group.

Bangladesh

In April 1982, the government of Bangladesh set up an expert committee to evaluate all the drugs registered and licensed in the country and to formulate a national drugs policy which would reflect the health needs of the country. In June of that year, the Ministry of Health accepted the recommendations of the expert committee as the national drugs policy. Based upon agreed criteria, 150 essential drugs were identified as adequate for most therapeutic purposes and another list of 100 supplementary drugs needed for tertiary level facilities was created. Over 1,500 drugs were withdrawn and an immediate ban was placed on 237 drugs considered harmful. Eight multinationals controlled 75 per cent of the market and their reaction was strongly negative. The industry's campaign to discredit and have the policy repealed was carried out principally on two levels (Rolt, 1985).

First, the industry sponsored a misinformation campaign directed at the medical establishment and the innumerable drugs sellers in the country. The self-styled medical journal financed by the drugs industry, *The Pulse*, ran numerous front page attacks on the policy. *The Pulse* is a medium for drugs advertising and has minimal medical value. At the time, 10,000 copies of the magazine were published every week and distributed free of charge to doctors by the industry's representatives. In editorials ranging from 'Most drugs banned not harmful' and 'Drug policy now a total failure' to 'Shortage of right medicines spread cholera and other diseases', the magazine orchestrated a campaign of disseminating inaccurate horror stories and misleading and incorrect information to doctors and drugs sellers, many of whom believed the worst in the absence of a similar concerted effort by the government to argue its case. The industry's representatives reinforced the misinformation by suggesting to doctors that their companies were withdrawing some popular products as a statement against the policy. In truth, these products had been withdrawn from the market because of their ineffectiveness.

Secondly, the multinationals lobbied their home governments to exert political and economic pressures upon the government of Bangladesh. In 1974, when the country's president, Sheik Mujib, had tried to introduce centralized drugs procurement from the cheapest source (Soviet bloc or China), the US had threatened to cut off food aid and the idea had to be dropped. Many in Bangladesh remembered this. The US, British and German ambassadors were most voluble and forceful in their criticisms of the policy and the US State Department spoke of its statutory responsibility to assist US interests abroad. It was also implied that the policy could well inhibit further investment in the country. Foreign diplomats suggested that the policy went against the Foreign Investment Protection Act and that as soon as martial law was lifted, the government would be taken to court over the issue. In one particular instance regarding the withdrawal of a certain product manufactured and sold by the US multinational, Pfizer, the final notice to the company from the Drugs Regulatory Board was responded to not by the company but, surprisingly, by the 'highest authority' in the government (the President's Office), letting the company off the hook by having the withdrawal notice itself withdrawn. Suggestively, a few days later, the president of Bangladesh and a group of his generals all flew to the US to meet President Reagan, followed by a tour of major US bases in South East Asia (Rolt, 1985).

The case of the Philippines (Tan, 1988) also illustrates how the US government supports its drugs multinationals by putting pressure on countries that attempt to develop rational drugs policies. The Aquino government's attempt to develop a national and rational drugs policy resulted in the US Chamber of Commerce in the Philippines and the Drug Association of the Philippines (25 corporate groups controlling about 80 per cent of the market in the country) submitting their own position papers on the subject. The Drug Association issued cryptic warnings about the loss of foreign investment in the drugs *and other* industries if the drugs policy attempted any sort of control. Gunboat diplomacy soon became the name of the game and a letter to President Aquino from US senators, Cranston and Lugar (major sponsors of a 'mini Marshall Plan' for the Philippines), urged her 'to look carefully at plans announced by [her] Minister of Health to implement a national drugs policy in the Philippines.' The letter (Tan, 1988) went on to say that 'if decisions are made which jeopardize or penalize US firms presently doing business in the Philippines, the task of stimulating new US investment may become more difficult'.

The launching of WHO's essential drugs list in 1977 and the creation of DAP in 1978 forced the industry onto the defensive. The essential drugs concept had been overwhelmingly endorsed at the WHA and continuing to fight it openly could only harm the industry's self-defined image as the world's provider of health. A damage limitation strategy was necessary and if it could be held to have a propaganda value, then all the better. Thus, while continuing the subtle campaign to discredit the essential drugs concept, the industry adopted a parallel strategy. It offered to support the concept by collaborating with WHO in setting up an EDP in a country to be jointly identified. Three Swiss-based multinationals, Roche, Sandoz and Ciba-Geigy, formed a consortium called Interpharma, and Burundi was chosen for the manifestation of the industry's contribution to the essential drugs concept. Other industry-sponsored programmes were implemented in The Gambia (the PMA, the US-based Pharmaceutical Manufacturers Association), the Maldives (Association of British Pharmaceutical Industry), Pemba Island (Tanzania) and Kenya (German Pharma Health).

Burundi

In 1980 WHO and Interpharma carried out a joint analysis of the drugs situation in Burundi. Concentrating on logistics and production, they paid little or no attention to a drugs policy or to the government's wish to implement any such policy. Interpharma sent an economist to Burundi to develop a project and the one Interpharma and Burundi eventually agreed to also failed to mention policy development.

Between 1982 and 1989 the Interpharma consultant made 14 trips to Burundi. Until 1983, however, Interpharma had spent only US$6,500 on the project and by 1985, after eight trips by the consultant, Interpharma's financial contribution totalled US$14,300 (Bannenberg, 1989). The consortium produced four glossy reports between 1982 and 1985, always in time for distribution at the WHA. Although to all intents and purposes WHO had withdrawn from the project, the reports always implied a joint WHO/Interpharma collaborative effort. These reports consisted mainly of planned activities awaiting funding, for Interpharma allegedly had insufficient funds to implement them. This is surprising considering that all three participants in the consortium were among the top 15 pharmaceutical companies (in terms of sales) in the world (SCRIP, 1986; SCRIP, 1987). In 1986 the Swiss Development Agency agreed to co-finance the project with about US$300,000 and, by 1987, Interpharma's total investment had increased to about the same amount.

An external evaluation of the project in 1987 (Berthoud, 1987) concluded that there was no clear drugs policy and that the essential drugs list contained many patent and non-essential items. Most of the money had been spent on warehouse improvement and vehicles. It added that the evaluation had been hindered because no clear aims or targets had been set for the project, base-line description was lacking and no concrete plans had been defined.

With the support of their governments multinationals have been able to influence local production by national companies. Whereas in Bangladesh, implementing the drugs policy enabled national companies to increase their share from 35.4 per cent in 1981 to 58.6 per cent in 1987 (for 45 essential drugs this increase was from 30.3 per cent to 74.8 per cent), economic developments in Colombia allowed the multinationals to strengthen their control to the detriment of local producers (Hansen et al., 1989). Western investment in Colombia was conditioned by the provision of incentives, which included tax exemptions, government subsidies for the installation of plants, low customs duty on raw materials and equipment, obligatory imports of intermediate goods from parent companies and profit repatriation facilities. The result was a dramatic fall in the amount of drugs produced by national manufacturers from a high of 55 per cent of the market in 1955 to 25 per cent in 1960, 10 per cent in 1970 and 4 per cent in 1975. The present figure is estimated to be around 15 per cent, with the other 85 per cent controlled by 40 multinationals.

In summary, the industry opposed the introduction of rational policies mainly through concern about the potential curtailment of its profits and an ideological belief in the free market. It needed an irrational pharmaceutical environment within countries to continue making enormous and unjustifiable profits. The adoption and implementation of an essential drugs policy meant rationalizing a chaotic sector. Each component of the policy was based on needs as opposed to demand and, therefore, from the industry's viewpoint, was a threat. The application of essential drugs lists, particularly to the private sector, would make the bulk of the industry's marketed products obsolete. Similarly, centralized procurement through international tenders would cut the ground away from the industry's practice of making deals with influential individuals, as well as professional groups such as doctors and pharmacists. Training and educating health workers and informing the public would break the industry's monopoly over 'scientific information'. The production and use of generic, as opposed to patent drugs attracted particular hostility from the industry because patent rights allowed it to charge high prices for its products for anywhere between 10 and 25 years. Countries such as Indonesia, Colombia, Thailand and the Philippines, which are capable of producing their own drugs, are being put under pressure from the US (aid or no aid being the stakes) to reactivate or introduce legislation to protect foreign patents.

The World Health Organization

The establishment of DAP in WHO created a structure within the organization that developing countries could contact and call upon for assistance in improving their drugs supply systems. From 1983 onwards, DAP, the organizational unit of APED, embarked upon a concerted campaign of advocacy for the essential drugs concept. It identified as priority those countries whose governments expressed a political will to rationalize their drugs policies, those where there was a need and those where there was a possibility of success. In its work DAP could only respond to requests made by countries, but when these were made its response was usually swift. The strategy DAP adopted was to work with interested countries in developing EDPs, often in limited geographical areas, then to capitalize on the improved procurement and distribution of drugs by helping the countries develop national policies based on the essential drugs concept. Though EDPs have been implemented in many countries with WHO assistance, these have generally focused on specific aspects of the supply system and have rarely provided a catalyst for the development of policy. Where government will is present, WHO's support can be critical.

People's Democratic Republic of Yemen (PDRY)

The PDRY's request for assistance in developing a 'medical supplies programme' gave WHO an opportunity to introduce the concept of an essential drugs policy into the Mediterranean region with a programme which might act as a catalyst for other countries in the region. The first WHO mission to the country included the DAP programme manager. After discussions with national policy-makers, a crucial conceptual change was made to the original programme proposal, i.e. developing a national drugs policy became its main objective.

WHO's financial support of the programme was critical, not only because of the amount of funds it made available (US\$761,194 from 1984-7), but also in that it provided untied money for crucial staff training and supplies. A close relationship developed between WHO's Eastern Mediterranean Regional Office and the committed programme staff in PDRY, who received strong government support.

Perhaps WHO's most important contributions to policy development in PDRY were in the technical support its consultants provided and in the awarding of 34 fellowships to cover every aspect of a national drugs policy. All those who received fellowships were still working at the posts for which they were trained some two years later. This comprehensive training strategy financed by WHO created a certain self-sufficiency for PDRY in terms of personnel (Kanji, 1989). A 1988 evaluation of the national programme found that, of a total of 216 recommendations by various consultants on all aspects of policy development, 72 per cent had been implemented and that a further 10 per cent were likely to be implemented in the forthcoming months (MOH/WHO, 1988). Such inputs, however, are not always sustainable and the recent amalgamation of Democratic Yemen with the YAR, with its different drugs policy, is likely to undermine WHO's work.

WHO's role has not always been this exemplary. When Bangladesh was trying to stand up to the pressures on its drugs policy, the local WHO representative refused either to applaud or condemn the new policy, even though the promotion of generic drugs was crucial to the government's attempt to consolidate its drugs policy. A local manufacturing company, Gonashasthaya Kendra, approached the WHO office in Dacca for permission to translate and distribute the WHO essential drugs list to convince doctors and pharmacists of the scientific validity of the essential drugs concept and the acceptability of generic drugs. The company also requested funding from WHO for this project. WHO replied that no funds were available for such an undertaking. However, it took WHO eight months to deny permission to translate the document on the grounds that Gonashasthaya Kendra was not a government organization. In fact the company later learned that WHO publications are not subject to copyright and so no permission was required in the first place (Chowdhury and Chowdhury, 1982). At a time when the Bangladesh drugs policy was under considerable attack, WHO's attitude could have been much more supportive, especially given that the country was trying to implement what DAP was promoting. Correct information about the copyright situation could have been promptly provided and the funds for translating could easily have been arranged.

WHO's role was also criticized in Mozambique. Here, in the face of increased dependence on donors, the government had been struggling to maintain its drugs policy by arguing in favour of maintaining and developing its state procurement company's expertise (confirmed by various independent consultants) in procuring good quality generic drugs on the international market. WHO insisted, however, that the drugs for the EDP should be purchased through the UNICEF supplies division (UNIPAC) and that MEDIMOC (the state company) should not canvass independent suppliers (Kanji, 1989). This was seen by many as an indirect attack on the country's policy and contradictory to WHO's intention to strengthen and sustain national capability.

A global analysis of WHO's role in individual countries (LSHTM/KIT, 1989), however, shows that its ability to attract funds for country programmes, either as 'seed money' to initiate activities or for full financial support from donors, was thought to have been useful. The technical support given in the form of consultants, guidelines, workshops, evaluations and training was also judged favourably by the countries concerned. Guidelines and other information were thought to be useful and the quality of consultants high. However, providing technical assistance was by no means the only way in which WHO was useful to the countries. The 1989 external evaluation of DAP concluded that 'governments attempting to rationalize their drugs systems face enormous political and economic pressures from various interests, national and international, and WHO's role as a global specialist agency providing political, moral and financial support to these countries is critical' (LSHTM/KIT, 1989).

Donors

The involvement of donors in the drugs field has to a certain extent been defined by the strength of their own drugs industry. On the whole, US, Swiss, German and Japanese aid agencies have been negative about the essential drugs concept and, where they have supported drugs programmes, the support has tended to reinforce their vested interests. The US, Switzerland, Germany and Japan all have large and powerful drugs industries and their lobbying power and influence over government policy is significant. The Italian pharmaceutical industry is large but not a major exporter and, through cooperation with the Italian aid agency, has managed to become an important supplier of essential drugs to country programmes supported by the Italian government.

The French industry is much more powerful and has a monopoly of supplying drugs to Francophone countries. The French government has facilitated this by enabling many Francophone countries to convert their currency directly into French francs. This means that these countries buy virtually all their drugs from France. Thus, although France was the first country to donate funds to DAP in 1980/1, since then its financial contribution has been modest. British support of the essential drugs concept has been mixed. It has given reasonable financial support to WHO's action programme, yet insufficient to bring about a particularly negative response from British industry, which is large and influential.

The Danish, Swedish and Dutch drugs industries are substantially smaller and have less influence over government decisions. In addition, these countries have longstanding social democracies with the state playing an important role in maintaining acceptable balances between private encouragement and public responsibility. They have been much more supportive of the essential drugs concept at the international level and, in their support of national programmes, have tended to aid policy development and ensure that drugs programmes are integrated into a wider and more comprehensive PHC strategy. Thus they have tended to see the availability of essential drugs as *one* aspect of a strategy that aims, not only to make primary level services more accessible to people, but also to improve their socio-economic and environmental conditions. Such donors have tried to avoid setting up EDPs that become ends in themselves through being implemented in a vertical manner with little or no horizontal integration with other health programmes within a wider health strategy. It is not, however, always possible to avoid the vertical implementation of programmes, with little or no horizontal integration with other health programmes.

Tanzania

In 1983, the Danish International Development Agency (DANIDA) agreed to finance an EDP in Tanzania, with a grant of US$30 million for the period 1984-6. The money was to be channelled through UNICEF, which would be the implementing agency. Supplying drugs to rural primary level facilities was identified as the main objective and activities were focused on procuring drugs kits from UNIPAC in Copenhagen and distributing them to the zonal stores in Tanzania. So seriously did UNICEF take this objective that, within a very short time, the pilot programme had become a national programme run from the UNICEF office, with an expatriate programme manager and four expatriate experts (Kanji et al., 1989). The Ministry of Health (MOH) did little to integrate these expatriates, or the programme, into the health system. The acute shortage of essential drugs all over rural Tanzania had reached crisis point and UNICEF, concentrating on the logistics of getting drugs out to the health facilities, managed to improve dramatically the availability of drugs for primary level services. However, this was only made possible by creating a vertical programme and a parallel distribution system.

Both DANIDA and the MOH expressed concern about the vertical implementation of the programme and its logistics focus. The MOH adopted a non-authoritative stance and, instead of coordinating donor input and defining how the programme should be implemented, left the initiative for changing the focus of the programme and integrating it into a PHC structure mainly to DANIDA. In the absence of any clear direction from the MOH, DANIDA and UNICEF took opposing views on how to implement the programme. The Programme Management Committee (PMC), comprising the MOH, DANIDA (Copenhagen), UNICEF (New York), WHO (Geneva) and the local DANIDA and UNICEF missions, which had been set up to define policy and strategy for the programme, could only reach decisions by consensus and, as this was often lacking, many necessary decisions were not taken.

DANIDA, ultimately responsible to the Danish parliament for how Danish aid is spent and controlled, defined its role as more than just a funder and wished to participate actively in the programme. UNICEF, however, saw the programme as a multilateral one in which it was the sole external executing agency. The tension resulting from these opposing points of view finally came to a head with DANIDA threatening to pull out of the programme. Eventually a compromise was reached in which the programme was split into two parts. The drugs programme became one of the units of a PHC department in the MOH, technically supported by DANIDA with six advisers, while UNICEF's role was limited to procurement and distribution, but working specifically with the central warehouse.

The MOH was reorganized with the chief medical officer (CMO) in charge of all operational aspects. The CMO thus became a powerful influence in the development of policy. Four of the six Danish advisers (in charge of senior management, finance, planning and the project), through the positions they occupied in the MOH and because some of them were co-signatories to the use of Danish funds, found themselves in positions of great influence. Danish participation in developing policy was effectively formalized. This, in addition to the advisers working very closely with the CMO, led to tensions between the CMO and the Principal Secretary (PS).

Matters came to a head in early 1990 when the PS refused to extend the contracts of the senior management, financial and planning advisers. In response, DANIDA froze the project funds and a stalemate was reached. The situation was eventually resolved when the PS was replaced in June 1990 (earlier, in March, the minister had also been replaced) and the contracts of the advisers renewed. Danish funds became available again. Many in Tanzania saw this episode as a clear example of donor conflicts and donor influence in affecting national policy.

In summarizing the role of donors in the 13 countries studied, the DAP evaluation (LSHTM/KIT, 1989) states that 'donor funds have been crucial to the development of essential drugs policies in these countries'. Though the

Tanzanian example above illustrates how DANIDA tried (and partially succeeded) to integrate its support for the EDP into a wider support for PHC, the DAP evaluation concludes that 'drug programmes have generally been implemented in a vertical fashion, establishing parallel supply, training and supervision systems. Where multiple drugs programmes are being implemented by various donors, coordination with and between donors has been difficult, resulting in the fragmentation of services and duplication of effort'.

UNICEF

UNICEF's main contribution to the EDPs has been in procuring essential drugs for country programmes through its supplies unit, UNIPAC. In 1988 US$36.6 million worth of drugs was purchased through UNIPAC. An evaluation of UNIPAC's drugs procurement procedures and practices (SGS, 1989) stated that its prices compared favourably with those of the world market. Evidence from other countries (Mozambique, Democratic Yemen, Bangladesh), however, suggests that they manage better prices and delivery times than UNIPAC can offer if they tender from a range of countries (Kanji, 1988; MOH/WHO, 1988).

Though UNICEF's involvement in drugs programmes has often helped improve national procurement (or more pertinently distribution systems), the tendency has been to execute these aspects through UNICEF project officers. The extent to which donor supported EDPs create parallel structures within a country is primarily dependent upon the government's ability to coordinate outside aid and take a clear lead in directing the development of the programmes. In the absence of such direction from the government, as in Tanzania, the vacuum is often filled by donors. The case of Mozambique, described below, shows that clear policy and direction by government is essential in ensuring that aid works to the constructive development of the country's health policy rather than duplicating efforts and fragmenting programmes. In 1987 UNICEF's focus shifted somewhat from supply and distribution to policy. This coincided with the launching of the Bamako Initiative, which arose from WHO's AFRO committee meeting in Bamako, Mali. The debate surrounding this initiative is dealt with in Chapter 2.

The above examples show the types of international actors and influences that can affect national drugs policy development. More often than not these actors behave in different ways at different times and in different combinations. Their activities are also often complemented by those of national actors who at various times find it convenient and/or necessary to align themselves with the interests of the international players.

The National Connection

It would be naïve and inaccurate to lay *all* power and influence at the doorstep of the international agencies. Such an analysis ignores the class dimension of what is essentially a politico-economic struggle for control and distribution of wealth.

An important determining factor in developing rational drugs policies has been the political and thus economic ideologies of the countries concerned. The fundamental issue revolves around two interrelated principles: how far the state accepts that its citizens have a basic right to health, upheld in laws that redistribute income and resources; and how far the state accepts that the private sector plays a major role in providing health care (and the extent to which the state regulates the private sector). Drugs play a central role in this debate because (a) their availability within a country is often regarded as an indication of the credibility of the health system and (b) the production, distribution and sale of drugs is immensely profitable for national and international companies, as well as for doctors, pharmacists and often even politicians, who are frequently part owners of drugs companies and retail pharmacies.

In countries where national health systems are central, the state has a dominant role and, in general, health is regarded as a right. Within such countries, the introduction and implementation of rational drugs policies has been easier because of the non-existent or relatively small private health sector.

Mozambique

The health system inherited at independence in 1975 reflected the economic and social characteristics of a colonial and oppressive system. The drugs market was characterized by total dependence on imports from five countries through 31 private importers. The illegal transfer of capital through over-invoicing or paying commissions to real or fictitious intermediaries was common, as was the proliferation of useless and dangerous medicines: 26,000 products were registered with about 13,000 in circulation. Expensive, sophisticated and dangerous products could be bought over the counter (MOH Mozambique, 1984).

One month after independence the health system was nationalized and, two months later, a Technical Commission of Therapeutics and Pharmacy was set up to produce the first National Drugs Formulary and the country's pharmaceutical policy, the principal components of which were:

The National Formulary: The first edition published in 1976 listed 430 drugs by generic names. The second edition of 1980 reduced this number to 343 and the 1984 edition contained 323 drugs. This last edition combined the formulary with the therapeutics guide and introduced a system of number codes specifying the category of health cadre and facility authorized to prescribe and use each drug.

Generic names: The use of generic names is obligatory at all levels of the health service and the training programmes for health cadres have assured this objective.

Centralized importation: In 1977 the state company, MEDIMOC, was created to allow the government progressively to centralize all drugs imports. Eighteen months later MEDIMOC became the sole importer of all pharmaceutical products by quoting prices between 10 and 20 times lower than those of other importers and putting them out of business. The government had thus attacked not the importers, but the structure of the drugs market.

Rational distribution: The national health service (NHS) was supplied through two regional stores. Provincial depots ensured that the correct drugs were distributed to each district.

In 1977, another state company (FARMAC) was created to take over the private pharmacies abandoned by the exodus of the Portuguese at independence. There are currently about 60 retail pharmacies and they also purchase their drugs from MEDIMOC. The retail prices are fixed by the state and allow a high profit margin, part of which is used to subsidize the NHS. To ease distribution to the rural areas, about 400 commercial establishments were authorized to sell a restricted number of drugs and first-aid material without prescription.

An economic evaluation of the drugs policy in 1983 showed that from 1976-82 Mozambique spent between 10 and 17 per cent of its health budget on drugs but, more importantly, it managed to quadruple the quantity of drugs imported without a significant increase in foreign currency spending. In addition, the NHS's share of the drugs budget increased from 28 per cent in 1977 to 61 per cent in 1982 (81 per cent in 1985). This significant increase in the availability of drugs for the NHS allowed for a higher coverage of the population in the rural areas; the number of primary level facilities increased from 446 in 1975 to 1,175 in 1982. The international tendering system also allowed the country to move away from a dependence on five countries for all its drugs. In 1982, drugs for the NHS were imported from 15 countries, none of which controlled more than 17 per cent of the market.

The international economic crisis, South African backed destabilization and natural disasters led to a dramatic downturn in Mozambique's economy. In 1985 only 55 per cent of the 1980 value of drugs was available and drugs shortages became frequent at all levels of the health service. Donations in kind, which up to 1982 had been a helpful adjunct to the system, suddenly became vital and introduced a new set of problems. Sending pharmaceuticals without prior discussion with the government resulted in the arrival of drugs that were not in the formulary, drugs that were included in the UN list of dangerous drugs and thus prohibited for use in Mozambique, as well as drugs that had already expired. The MOH took a strong position and prohibited the circulation of these products and, in a concerted action with the Ministry of Foreign Affairs, contacted the various embassies and agencies involved to explain the country's drugs policy. These efforts paid off, for whereas only 37 per cent of the drugs received in 1983 had been 'useful', this had risen to 74 per cent by 1985 (Cliff et al., 1986).

The ever increasing dependence on aid led the MOH to work out a strategy that would not only guarantee the availability of the 103 products it defined as vital but would also uphold the country's policy. Maintaining MEDIMOC's expertise by asking donors to channel their funds through the company so that it could carry on the efficient procurement of drugs was a central part of this strategy. Sweden, The Netherlands and West Germany sent their consultants to evaluate MEDIMOC's procedures and practices. All of them recommended that MEDIMOC should indeed carry out the procurement. When in 1987, USAID donated US$3.4 million channelled through UNICEF for drugs purchases, most people assumed that the drugs would be bought through UNIPAC. The MOH successfully argued that, in comparison with MEDIMOC, UNIPAC prices were high and delivery times long and that, instead of automatically supplying the drugs, UNIPAC should bid alongside other suppliers in an international tender to be carried out by MEDIMOC. Mozambique's clear policy and the will to back it even from a position of economic weakness had paid off (Kanji, 1988).

Any national policy is subject to outside influences. In Mozambique the drugs policy could easily have been fragmented and diluted by donors had the government not fought back and taken the initiative in involving the many donors in supporting the government to maintain its policy. In Bolivia, described below, commercial interests within the country with partnerships outside and a weak MOH were what managed to have the drugs policy overturned.

Bolivia

When the democratic coalition came to power in 1982 after 20 years of direct and indirect military rule, it inherited a serious economic and social crisis. Prudencio and Tognoni (1987) describe the situation and the government's efforts to implement a rational drugs policy. With only the regularly employed (about 28 per cent) covered by some form of social security, with approximately a third of the population without access to health care, with 60 per cent of the health budget spent on drugs for only about 40 per cent of the population and with immense speculation in national and international drugs transactions, the new government assigned top priority to reforming the drugs situation in the country. Between 1977 and 1982 it embarked on a process of rationalization by establishing a therapeutics committee to produce a national formulary and an essential drugs list. The country depended heavily, however, on importing finished products (70 per cent); local production accounted for only 30 per cent of the market and was concentrated in about 15 plants with a total labour force of less than 1,000 workers. Liberal trading conditions encouraged an overpricing practice that was tantamount to capital flight and of great benefit to the importers (ASOFAR). In addition, the importers and producers (ALIFABOL) wholly controlled the distribution network, not only through sales to private pharmacies but, more importantly, through tenders to the NHS. 'The state was therefore at the origin of the financing providing hard currency to the importers in the private sector. It also supported the sector through payments made to the only institutions through which drugs could be reimbursed' (Prudencio and Tognoni, 1987).

The new government saw health as a basic human right and gave priority to establishing a PHC system. It also saw a stronger role for the state in the economy and realized that if there were to be social gains some of the excessive imports that facilitated capital flight would need to be controlled. Drugs were an obvious area for reform and, as part of the strategy to achieve it, a central agency (INASME) was set up to revise the national formulary, procure essential drugs and ensure their availability throughout the country. It was hoped that after a transitional phase INASME would replace the importers' association (ASOFAR) and take over the importing of raw materials from the producers' association (ALIFABOL). Starting with a pilot project to import directly 150 generic drugs, within a short period of 15 months, the policy had shown that essential drugs could be procured efficiently for the majority of the population at a mere 10 per cent of the pre-policy cost. Moreover, a mark-up in the net cost of importing made it possible to employ technical staff, set-up six regional pharmacies as distribution points for the PHC network and run seminars to update the national formulary.

From its inception, INASME incurred the wrath of the pharmaceutical industry and private pharmacists who, seeing a threat to their profits, embarked on a systematic campaign to discredit the policy by circulating rumours about the poor quality of the INASME generic drugs. The revision of the formulary was presented as a 'threat to scientific development and to the country's health rights' (Prudencio and Tognoni, 1987). The debate on whether health is a right or a commodity found varied opinions, with open opposition to the policy from the Ministry of Industry and Commerce and the Ministry of Planning, who interpreted the MOH's policy as an incursion into 'their domain'. ALIFABOL thus found natural allies within the coalition government. These conflicts delayed the budgetary allocations for INASME and this affected its capacity to meet procurement deadlines and develop its distribution network. The increasingly uncontrolled economic and social conditions aggravated the situation and the policy began to lose some of its credibility. (In 15 months during 1984/5, the inflation rate soared from 300 per cent to 1,900 per cent.)

The return to power of the previous oligarchy in August 1985 put the final nail in the coffin. Two months later INASME was disbanded and economic policies giving priority to the liberalization of imported goods (including drugs) and prices and to the 'adjustment' of the labour market were the order of the day. Health had once again become a commodity to be purchased by those able to afford it.

Conflicts such as those in Bolivia are not uncommon. The different objectives of and differences of opinion between the MOH and the Ministry of Trade and Industry (MTI) have been important factors in impeding the development of a rational drugs policy in Tanzania. The MTI is guided by principles of profit and its parastatal importing company, NAPCO, imports many non-essential but profit-making items, which are distributed not only through private pharmacies but also through NAPCO's own chain of retail pharmacies. NAPCO and the MTI have therefore been opposed to any policy that might reduce these profits. Take, too, the case of the YAR, now part of unified Yemen, which is not itself unique in the following aspect. In the YAR public sector doctors also engage in private practice and have a vested interest in the sale of drugs. About 90 per cent of the pharmacists in the government sector have an interest in the private sector, either through running private pharmacies or through being employed as part-time representatives for the drugs companies. These are the very people who would be responsible for conceptualizing and implementing a potential rational drugs policy. With low salaries in the public sector and frequent and often substantial kickbacks to health professionals and government officials from interested parties, it is difficult to see how a rational policy could develop in the country. Given that the YAR has a much larger population and drugs market than Democratic Yemen, their union in 1991 possibly augers badly for the maintenance of the rational drugs policy in Democratic Yemen.

Chemists and druggists in India exercised their power in 1979 when the government introduced a new drugs policy. Its attempt to reduce the prices of essential drugs by cutting profit margins to 40-50 per cent resulted in the producers ceasing production and the retailers not stocking the items (Greenhalgh, 1987). A price constraint on essential drugs also meant that the production of non-essential ones increased to maintain profit levels. Similarly, when attempts were made to restrict the sale of psychotropic drugs by putting them on prescription, the druggists responded with a boycott. The drugs ceased to be stocked and epileptics and psychiatric patients had enormous problems obtaining them. The government's decision to restrict the sale of drugs to trained and qualified pharmacists caused a three-day total national strike (Shiva, 1985). In 1975, the Hathi Committee had made two major recommendations for improving the drugs problem in India: the first was to nationalize the drugs industry and reduce foreign investors' equity to 40 per cent initially and later to 26 per cent (India produces almost all its drugs locally) and the second was to introduce the phased abolition of brand names and all new single ingredient products sold under generic name. But 15 years later, in 1990, little had happened. The drugs companies had found various loopholes in the legislation and, together with the pressure exerted by their governments on India, had created a stalemate, with the matter still pending in the Indian courts (Rolt, 1985).

In Bangladesh a significant proportion of the largely urban literate minority of bureaucrats and businessmen opposed the new drugs policy introduced in 1982. Francis Rolt graphically describes how sections of this minority, identifying strongly with Western consumer habits, mounted an aggressive misinformation campaign in the press (which they owned) to create confusion and discredit the policy (Rolt, 1985). Two pro-US national papers described the policy as an attack on US business interests and actively campaigned against it. An effective mixture of stories concentrating on how the shortage of drugs was creating a black market in the country and cryptic references to 'neo-colonial conspiracies' to inhibit and destroy local enterprise had the desired effect on the public. The government itself did little to explain and disseminate its policy. Rumours, carefully initiated and subtly propagated, implied that the policy had made the West unwilling to invest in the country, had resulted in an increase in the smuggling of banned drugs and had caused the proliferation of spurious drugs.

The 'commodity' characteristic of drugs is thus important not only to multinational and national manufacturers and interested Western governments, but also to the professionally organized and class-based groupings within the countries in question. Many representatives of these groups earn their livings by prescribing and selling drugs and, as seen above, are powerful and influential enough to oppose vehemently any policy that affects their economic status.

Kenya, one of the bastions of a free market economy, exemplifies the sort of accommodation often made between health as a right and health as a commodity and the interests that influence policy.

Kenya

In the decade following the war of independence in Kenya in the 1950s, Britain concentrated on creating a black national middle class to safeguard its economic and political interests in the country. At independence in 1963 this objective had been achieved and, with British and other capital, this class rapidly consolidated its power on the national political and economic scene.

Though there was an increase in the number of health facilities in the rural areas, this was achieved mainly by the private, non profit-making sector composed of religious and other non-governmental (mainly foreign) organizations. Private health boomed, as did the business in drugs. The rapid creation and consolidation of the black middle class was made possible by laws, one of which stipulated that every foreign company had to take on at least one Kenyan partner. In the drugs sector, therefore, an almost overnight vested interest was created for the national power holders, for these were the people who became the multinational industries' Kenyan partners and directors. The interests of international and national capitalists were thereby largely harmonized. For the multinationals this worked very well. While the national companies controlled the retail outlets and the production of certain generic and galenical products, they, the multinationals, had a guaranteed market for their patent protected products, which were used extensively in the private and public sectors.

As in many other countries, one effect of the economic crisis of the 1970s was a shortage of drugs in public health services, especially in the rural areas. The private sector, though relying on scarce foreign exchange to import drugs, faced no great problem, but the drugs available through this sector were too expensive for the majority of the population. In January 1981 the EDP was initiated under the New Management System of Drug Supplies (therefore independent of the rest of the drugs procurement and distribution system). The objective was to supply essential drugs in ration kits to rural primary-level health facilities. DANIDA and later SIDA agreed to cover the costs of the drugs, which were initially all purchased through UNIPAC and later partially supplied by local producers.

Since then, much has been written about the Kenyan experience in making essential drugs available to rural areas through the regular supply of ration kits. The experience has also been promoted as a model for other countries to follow. However, little has been said about the influence (or lack of) of this world famous programme on the development of a rational drugs policy in the country. Though Kenya has hosted a large number of international and regional conferences, workshops and seminars on almost all aspects of essential drugs, it is interesting that a *national* workshop on the essential drugs concept and comprehensive policy development in Kenya has never been organized. Perhaps this is not so surprising given the prevailing free market ideology and the powerful alliance between national and international entrepreneurs. In 1989 the annual turnover of the drugs market in Kenya was estimated at about US$60 million. The rationalized element, the EDP costing about US$11 million a year, represents only about 18 per cent of the national drugs market. This situation, with its continued preferential allocation of foreign currency to the private sector and the donors' shift towards funding district-level integrated PHC programmes (as opposed to vertical components of PHC) has led the donors, DANIDA and SIDA, to decide to withdraw from funding the programme.

Introducing changes to drugs policy is often complicated by the extent of local (national as opposed to international) production. Though seen as a way of making financial savings and becoming self-reliant, promoting local production creates economic and political problems by placing the local and international industries in a confrontational situation. From a health perspective this may well reduce the debate into a nationalist argument, with the key question of 'what is being produced and for whose benefit' remaining unanswered and often unasked. In Indonesia, for example, total drugs market sales are estimated at about US$456 million annually. There are about 287 registered manufacturers, of which 40 are transnationals, four are government owned and the rest belong to national entrepreneurs. The transnationals control 55 per cent of the market and the fierce competition between the producers encourages aggressive marketing techniques. On the other hand, there are 12,606 drugs registered in the country, with cases of over 100 patent products registered for one drug (LSHTM/KIT, 1989).

Though it may seem difficult to implement a national policy based upon the essential drugs concept, it is by no means impossible. What is crucial is the government's commitment to improve the health standards of the majority of its population. A positive role has to be found for both the national companies and the private health sector in developing rational drugs policies. Certainly compromise may have to be made in terms of which drugs are truly essential, but as long as the private sector curbs the excesses in its marketing strategies and allows the major proportion of health budgets (including drugs) to benefit the majority, there is no reason why a *modus vivendi* cannot be achieved. Perhaps the solution lies in defining more clearly the role of the private sector and the extent to which the state needs to regulate its activities.

Zimbabwe

The 15 years of unilateral independence for the white minority in Rhodesia, which many countries boycotted, not only created a heavy dependence upon South Africa, but also significantly developed local industry. One such development was a self reliant pharmaceutical industry. The health situation in the country was very poor for the rural subsistence farmers, slightly better for the urban working class and excellent for the whites, who used a well organized private health sector. At independence in 1980, the PHC approach was declared official government policy and a decentralized health care system based upon PHC concepts was initiated. Independence also brought a threefold increase in demand for health services, for people previously excluded from these services could now benefit from them. It was obviously necessary to set priorities, redistribute resources and rationalize policy, especially in the drugs field.

In 1981 the *Proposed Essential Drugs List of Zimbabwe* (PEDLIZ) was published; it was to be compulsory for the public sector and recommended for the private sector, which mainly ignored it. Health workers at all levels were asked to comment on the list (which they did) and, in 1985, EDLIZ was published. The following year the Essential Drugs Programme (ZEDAP) was made operational to tackle the many problems within the whole drugs supply system. ZEDAP adopted a 'bottom up' approach, which brought peripheral health workers into various national workshops to create realistic guidelines on the use of essential drugs. The health workers' commitment to the concept was thus developed and consolidated through their active participation. In addition, ZEDAP organized a national workshop on policy development, bringing together all concerned parties, including the private sector. The meeting was successful in preparing a national drugs policy, which the government endorsed. The participatory approach once again ensured that potential confrontation was channelled into useful contribution. With solid backing from the public sector, the government announced that, as from January 1990, the policy and the obligatory use of generic names would also apply to the private sector (Bannenberg, 1989a).

The German and Swiss pharmaceutical industries immediately sent delegations to Zimbabwe. The British Pharma Group, representing Beechams, Boots, Glaxo, ICI and Wellcome, sent a letter via the Zimbabwean High Commission to persuade the country to rethink its policy in the private sector because 'generics could never achieve the quality of the patent products'. The government seemed to stand firm. National producers and the private health sector appeared to be supporting the drugs policy. Zimbabwe did not nationalize the white owned industries at independence but instead sought a positive role for them in the development of the country. It thus bought a 42 per cent share in the previously private drugs producing company, CAPS, which also owns an important wholesaler and a chain of retail pharmacies. This, combined with preferential buying of drugs from local manufacturers and the fact that it controls the allocation of foreign currency to these manufacturers for the import of raw materials, was thought by many to ensure their passive, if not active, support for the government's policy. Thus, with the private sector potentially participating in the implementation of the policy, it was thought to be easier to withstand international pressure in that the issue was not a political one, but a question of the rational use of resources for the benefit of the majority. In September 1990, however, the legislation covering the private sector was still sitting on the new health minister's desk, unsigned. The private sector appears to have fought a strong rearguard action, possibly with support from various Western governments. Economic pressure must certainly have been brought to bear for the Zimbabwe government to have sat on the legislation for so long. It is now unlikely that the private sector will be totally subject to the country's drugs policy.

Finally, it is necessary to consider some of the constraints that developing countries face even when there is a political will to rationalize their drugs systems. Countries such as Bangladesh and Mozambique, which have rational drugs policies, face enormous infrastructral problems. Health coverage is low, storage and distribution of drugs precarious and economic conditions unfavourable. Increasing dependence on donors to provide drugs brings problems of a different nature, as we have seen. Health staff in the public sectors of these countries are frequently poorly trained and salaries are often insufficient to provide for basic necessities. Under such conditions, it is difficult to motivate staff in the rational use of drugs and leakages from the system are commonplace. A more worrying phenomenon is the appearance of fake drugs on the market. The extent of the problem and its lethal consequences for people's health jeopardizes many of the advances countries have achieved in their drugs systems. The Nigerian government recently tried to introduce a rational drugs policy, but in a country where up to 25 per cent of all drugs on the market are thought to be phoney or substandard (Masland and Marshall, 1990), it faces major problems.

In conclusion, a country's pharmaceutical and health policy cannot be isolated from its general development strategy. Good health depends on many factors and health services and drugs play only a limited part in improving health. A national development strategy aimed towards improving people's living conditions and, therefore, their health requires economic growth and its equitable distribution. This in turn depends not only on national factors but, perhaps more importantly, on international economic, financial and political conditions, which the developing world is often unable to affect. Ultimately, then, a country's pharmaceutical policy is open to manipulation by international influences, especially if the country is heavily dependent on aid and/or loans for financing its drugs costs.

The national élites controlling a country's political and economic spheres (and therefore its developmental direction) are key actors. Depending on their ideological positions or economic interests, they either ally themselves with international forces, thereby promoting the 'commodity' system within which rational policies have no place, or they embrace and implement rational policies, which invariably lead them into a confrontation with the industry and/or powerful Western interests. More often than not a compromise position is adopted in which the public sector is fully (rarely) or partially rationalized, but in which the private sector's enormous political influence and economic strength distorts the rationalization. Policies applied only to the public sector rationalize but a tiny proportion of the drugs market; not only is the rest of the market exempted from these policies, but often, through various incentives and subsidies, encouraged to develop further.

References

Bannenberg, W. (1989) 'Evaluation of WHO's APED'. *Burundi Desk Study*, London: LSHTM/KIT
———— (1989a) 'Evaluation of WHO's APED'. *Zimbabwe Desk Study*, London: LSHTM/KIT
Berthoud, S. (1987) *Projet pilote du Burundi: Rapport d'évaluation pour le compte d'Interpharma*. Geneva: Institute for Development Studies
Chowdhury, Z. and S. Chowdhury (1982) 'Essential drugs for the poor: Myth and reality in Bangladesh'. *Ecodevelopment News*, 23 December, Paris
Cliff, J., N. Kanji and M. Muller (1986) 'Mozambique health: Holding the line'. *Review of African Political Economy*, 36, 7-23
Greenhalgh, T. (1987) 'Drug prescription and self-medication in India: An exploratory survey'. *Social Science and Medicine*, 25 (3), 307-18
Hansen, J., J. Ramirez-Hernandez and V. Ruiz (1989) 'Evaluation of WHO's APED'. *Colombia Case Study*, London: LSHTM/KIT
Kanji, N. (1988) 'Drug policy and financing in Mozambique: Is the Bamako Initiative feasible?' Unpublished M.Sc. dissertation, LSHTM, University of London

—————— (1989) 'Evaluation of WHO's APED'. *Democratic Yemen desk study*, London: LSHTM/KIT

Kanji, N., M. Munishi and G. Sterky (1989) 'Evaluation of WHO's APED'. *Tanzania Case Study,* London: LSHTM/KIT

LSHTM/KIT (1989) *An evaluation of WHO's Action Programme on Essential Drugs.* London: LSHTM/KIT

Masland, T. and R. Marshall (1990) 'The pill pirates'. *Newsweek,* 5 November

MOH Mozambique (1984) *Para una politica de medicamentos.* Maputo: MOH

MOH/WHO (1988) *Evaluation of UNDP programme Democratic Yemen.* Geneva: WHO

Prudencio, I. and G. Tognoni (1987) 'Essential drugs policy in Bolivia'. *Health Policy and Planning,* 2 (4): 301-8

Rolt, F. (1985) *Pills, policies and profits.* London: War on Want

SCRIP No. 1166/7, 25 December 1986 and 1 January 1987

Shiva, M. (1985) 'Towards a healthy use of pharmaceuticals: An Indian perspective'. *Development Dialogue,* 2, 69-93

SGS (1989) *Evaluation of UNICEF's drug procurement procedures and practices.* Antwerp: Société Général de Surveillance

Tan, M. (1988) *Dying for drugs: Pill power and politics in the Philippines.* Quezon City, Philippines: HAIN

War on Want (1982) *Bangladesh: Finding the right prescription.* London: War on Want

WHO (1977) *The selection of essential drugs.* Geneva: WHO

—————— (1988) *Guidelines on national drug policies.* Geneva: WHO

5

What Has Been Achieved andWhere Are We Now?

Najmi Kanji and Anita Hardon

Chapter 4 looked at essential drugs policies and programmes at the country level and the dynamics of the various forces that influence national policy development. This chapter summarizes the data available on the impact of drugs policies and programmes in terms of the increased availability and rational use of essential drugs. It also assesses the achievements of WHO's Action Programme on Essential Drugs (DAP) during the 15 years of its existence.

In its progress report of May 1989, DAP gave an overview of what countries had achieved between 1983 and 1989 in adopting essential drugs lists (EDLs) and looked at the number of existing essential drugs programmes (EDPs) (WHO/APED, 1989).

Essential Drugs Lists

Figure 5.1 from the above report shows the growth in the number of countries with EDLs from 1983 to 1989.

Although the increase both in absolute and percentage terms is impressive, the figures have to be viewed with caution as certain crucial aspects of information are missing. The global evaluation of DAP in 1989 showed that EDLs existed in all the 12 countries studied. However, in seven of the countries the list only applied to the public sector, with the private sector exempt of any restriction on the type of drugs purchased, prescribed and sold (LSHTM/KIT, 1989). The relative values of the public and private sectors in the countries studied are shown in Table 5.1.

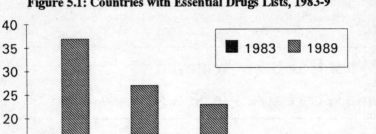

Figure 5.1: Countries with Essential Drugs Lists, 1983-9

Table 5.1: The Drugs Market from 13 Country Case Studies

Country	Market US$ 000s	Drug Ex/cap	Public (%)	Private (%)
Colombia	285,000	10.00		
Nigeria	n/a			
Tanzania	30,690	1.33	65	35
Kenya	50,000	2.36	32	68
Zimbabwe	21,500	2.47	70	30
Mozambique	6,878	0.60	81	19
Burundi	n/a			
Yemen (N)	65,000	7.92	8	92
Sudan	55,000	2.43		
Yemen (S)	14,200	6.45		
Bangladesh	122,700	1.18	13	87
Indonesia	456,000	2.74	17	83
Vietnam	30,000	0.47	100	0

Notes: (1) About US$30m worth of drugs said to enter Vietnam annually as 'gifts' is not included above. (2) The data were compiled at the following dates: 1984-South Yemen (PDRY); 1985-Colombia, Mozambique; 1986-Kenya; 1987-Tanzania, Bangladesh, Indonesia, Vietnam; 1988-Zimbabwe, North Yemen (YAR) and Sudan.

Source: LSHTM/KIT (1989)

The authors of the report state that the above figures should be 'interpreted with caution'. None the less, it is reasonably clear that the value of adopting an essential drugs list is limited if it is applied only to the public sector, which may command a much smaller proportion of drugs expenditure than the private sector. In some countries the EDL is not mandatory even for the public sector; for example, in Colombia it is only indicative. Furthermore, in some countries EDLs apply only to primary level services. The hospitals consuming the major part of the total drugs budget are often not obliged to adhere to these lists. In Indonesia legislation has been introduced to make the EDL mandatory for primary level services in the public sector, but it allows hospitals to use drugs not on the list and, on average, they use up to 25 per cent more than the listed drugs. The effectiveness of these lists is even more questionable when one considers that in Kenya the number of drugs registered for circulation in the country is 3,500, in Colombia 6,250 and in Indonesia 12,606 (LSHTM/KIT, 1989). Drugs regulatory authorities with the resources and power to enforce legislation and adherence to the drugs lists are either non-existent or ineffectual in all the above 12 countries.

Essential Drugs Programmes

The increase in the number of countries with existing EDPs, shown in Figure 5.2 below, should also be viewed with caution.

Figure 5.2: Countries with Operational EDPs, 1983 and 1989

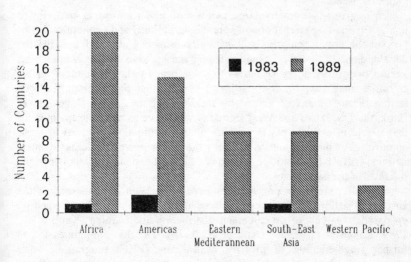

Rural primary level services were particularly badly hit by the economic crisis of the 1970s and 1980s and the resultant drugs shortages in developing countries, and this was partly because of the generally skewed allocation of resources in favour of urban hospitals. The rationale behind the implementation of EDPs was to give credibility to preventive and promotive services through the regular provision of essential drugs, thus providing examples that could later be emulated in a national, comprehensive drugs policy.

In practice, however, expectations have not been wholly lived up to. In many cases the drugs programmes have failed to venture out of their initial geographical areas and, where they have extended their coverage, the expansion has generally been confined to the public sector and primary level services. The external evaluation showed that, of the 13 countries studied, four had existing drugs policies before the implementation of the EDP and, of the remaining nine countries, a national policy covering both public and private sectors and all levels of health care, had developed in only one country (Democratic Yemen) as a result of an EDP. Zimbabwe appears to have decided against including the private sector in the country's legislation, though Tanzania seems now willing to move towards a comprehensive drugs policy.

The main reason why EDPs have not had more impact on the development of national policy within countries has been because of a lack of willingness among governments to restrict the use of inessential drugs and introduce restrictive legislation within the private sector. Certain conceptual and operational aspects of drugs programmes have also, however, influenced the issue.

First, given that a very large number of EDPs are either partially or totally funded by external donors, prevailing political and economic ideologies in the donor countries will naturally influence attitudes towards the development of policy. Scandinavian countries have on the whole been keener than other donor countries to see a drugs policy introduced in the countries they support. It is unlikely, though, that programmes financed (either through loans or grants) by the World Bank, Asian Development Bank, the US, Japan and West Germany will serve as catalysts for policies that would effectively cut the profits of the multinationals based in these countries. As these countries are also the major power wielders in international financial institutions, it becomes difficult to distinguish between the interests of the two groups.

Secondly, since the programmes have often been implemented in the absence of national policy they have tended to become vertical, often setting up parallel systems of procurement, distribution and training (Kanji et al., 1989; Lunde et al., 1989; Islam et al., 1989). This has sometimes led to further fragmentation of primary health care (PHC) programmes and unnecessary duplication of effort. Where there is no single national programme, the situation is often characterized by multiple programmes implemented in various parts of the country by different donors. The problem then is one of coordination with and between donors. In Bangladesh, for example, where a drugs policy exists, there are at least six different programmes related to drugs (Islam et al., 1989). These are (a) UNDP/WHO involved in the intensification of PHC activities; (b) UNICEF/SIDA supplying drugs and dietary supplement kits (DDS); (c) DANIDA/SIDA/WHO Essential Drugs Project; (d) Asian Development Bank Health and Family Services Project constructing stores for the storage of DDS and family planning kits *only*; (e) World Bank loan to purchase DDS kits from UNICEF; and (f) USAID construction of warehouses for storing drugs and contraceptives, mainly for family planning. This sort of uncoordinated aid weakens rather than strengthens a country's policy.

Thirdly, since many programmes are supplied with drugs kits (specified quantities of essential drugs based on morbidity data and packed in strong cardboard boxes to prevent pilferage and breakage), often through UNICEF's procurement division in Copenhagen (UNIPAC), undue focus can be placed on the logistics of the programme to the detriment of training and policy (Kanji et al., 1989). The kit system of supplying drugs was a real innovation and has certainly improved the regular availability of essential drugs for rural primary level services. Supplying kits, however, which was supposed to be a means of helping governments adopt rational drugs policies, has often become an end in itself. An enormous amount of energy is spent on refining the contents of the kits to avoid shortages and/or excesses of various items. Important as this is, a perfect kit is probably unattainable and trying to create one is not an important objective. Thus, valuable time is spent on deciding whether the kit should contain 3,000 or 4,000 aspirin tablets, while the more complex issues related to policy development are insufficiently stressed. In many of the programmes UNICEF is the disbursement agency. It holds the money from the donor and spends it after consultation with the government and the donor. This means that UNICEF internal spending and financial control systems have to be followed. These systems bear no relation to the government's management and financial systems and if the government wishes to monitor how *its* money being held by UNICEF is spent, officials have to learn the UNICEF system. This is daunting and if government officials do not understand the inner workings of UNICEF's systems, then financial monitoring becomes difficult. Control is effectively maintained by the donor organization.

Finally, it is necessary to mention the 'aid' aspect of drugs programmes. Interviews with various donors involved in this area revealed that the funding of drugs programmes, especially through an international agency, is viewed favourably by donors. This is because it makes both the donor and the recipient feel good about affecting people's health. It also often has positive spin-offs for the donor country's drugs industry and disbursement of funds is relatively easy, given that large sums can be utilized quickly with little technical expertise required within the donor agency. In the case of money channelled through UNICEF, the interest earned on the money reverts not to the recipient government or programme but to UNICEF. In

Tanzania, the interest from Danish funds for the EDP for the period 1984-6 amounted to US$2.2 million (Kanji et al., 1989). UNICEF's 'earnings' go into general funds to be used by the organization as it sees fit. In 1987, of UNIPAC's total purchases of US$155 million from the Copenhagen warehouse alone, drugs and vaccines amounted to US$83 million (53.5 per cent). The total amount of purchases, including those through New York, was US$213 million (UNICEF, 1988). By 1988, the total figure had increased to US$248.5 million (LSHTM/KIT, 1989). The question here is, do these sums of money create an environment in which drugs programmes keep buying their kits through UNIPAC rather than developing national procurement systems based on running international tenders by generic name? Seven years after its implementation the Tanzanian programme still buys kits through UNIPAC in Copenhagen, even though one of the original objectives of the programme was to develop national capabilities and systems in international drugs procurement.

The Availability of Essential Drugs

DAP's main aims have been to increase the availability of essential drugs for primary level services and to promote their rational use. The 1989 evaluation of the programme (LSHTM/KIT 1989) had this to say:

> Finally, evidence from these countries [13 country case studies] suggests that general availability of essential drugs at the primary level has been increased through regular supply. The accessibility of these drugs to people remains dependent on the health system's coverage. In comparison to the early 1980s, essential drugs are being purchased and distributed preferentially to primary level services. However, indications are that problems exist in the prescribing of drugs at all levels of the health system. Excessive use of antibiotics, injectables and vitamins is common. Where availability of essential drugs has increased, there appears to have been a corresponding increase in the credibility of the health services and morale of health workers. This has facilitated preventive and promotive health activities.

DAP's 1983 Global Medium Term Plan specified targets such as 'at least 20 essential drugs will be available to 80 per cent of the population, within one hour's walk, or travel, in 20 countries by the end of 1989'. Given that it is almost impossible to measure the achievement of such targets, such statements are more a reflection of intentions than objectives that can be evaluated.

   None the less, in countries where donor funds have been regularly available for the purchase of drugs and where improvements have been made in the logistics of supplying drugs (transport, storage and management), the availability of essential drugs for primary level health facilities appears to have improved. UNICEF claims that the Tanzania programme, for example, reaches 20 million rural Tanzanians. Table 5.2 below shows the distribution of drugs kits in six of the countries studied in the evaluation of DAP.

Table 5.2: Distribution of Essential Drugs to Primary Level Services

Country	Date	Units(no.)	Units(type)	Kits(no. p.a)
Democratic Yemen	1988	180	HCs	n/a
Kenya	1988	382	HCs	
		982	Ds	46,300
Tanzania	1987	300	HCs	
		2690	Ds	35,880
Mozambique	1988	221	HCs	
		720	HPs	
		475	VHWs	24,000*
Yemen Arab Republic	1988	368	HCs	
		273	PHCs	1,391
Sudan	1987	44	HCs	
		78	Ds	
		76	DSs	
		94	PHCs	3,240*

Notes: 1. * approximate figures
2. Figures for Sudan cover the Nile Province Project.
Key: HCs=Health Centres; Ds=Dispensaries; HPs=Health Posts; VHWS=Village Health Workers; PHCs=Primary Health Care units; DSs=Dressing Stations.
Source: LSHTM/KIT (1989); Evaluation of WHO's APED.

In 1989 DAP commissioned an evaluation of the kit drugs supply system, which concluded (Chetley, 1990) that greatly improved availability of drugs in rural health facilities is without doubt the most successful part of the kit system. The author suggested that one reason for this was that the kit system had usually been implemented in areas where drugs availability was very deficient. The system encouraged national and district level planners to focus attention on rural health care needs, with the net effect that there was increased confidence in the health system among both rural health workers and the public. The report did, however, point out two major disadvantages of the kit system: its difficulty in estimating requirements and its inflexibility. Country data also showed that shortages still existed. An analysis of the type of drugs most frequently reported in short supply suggested that, though shortages is some countries may be related to insufficient quantities in the kits, over-prescribing was at least a contributing factor. The system's shortcomings were especially apparent in long delivery times, interrupted supplies, dispatch of wrong kits and long lead time for changes in the kit content.

The Rational Use of Drugs

Increasing the availability of drugs and enhancing their rational use are two interrelated aims. Without essential drugs being available, their rational use cannot be achieved. This means not only that appropriate drugs are prescribed, but that they are available when needed and at a price people can afford; that they are taken in the right dose, at the right intervals and for the right length of time; and that they are effective, of acceptable quality and safe. Providing the general public and health workers at all levels of the health care system with continuous training and regular information are preconditions for rational drugs use. It is in this area of work that gaps and weaknesses have been identified in the implementation of EDPs and policies. Without appropriate educational strategies rational drugs use cannot be expected. A review of the countries covered in the evaluation reveals that training and/or information is inadequate in all of them. In Tanzania and Kenya crash training courses for middle and lower level health workers have been organized, but these have not been satisfactorily followed up. Both these countries, as well as Vietnam, Sudan and Mozambique have a manual for health workers, but there is no supervision of its use. In some countries, such as Kenya and Bangladesh, attempts have been made to develop ways of educating the general public, but these have not led on to more general activities in the field of information provision or education.

What emerges from the country reports is that, despite the millions of dollars spent on formulating and implementing essential drugs policies world-wide, the impact of these activities depends a great deal on how rationally drugs are being used and this has not been systematically evaluated.

Assessing Rational Drugs Use

Looking at prescribing practices in government health care centres seems to be the most obvious way of measuring the rational use of drugs. It is through these centres that governments intend to increase the availability of essential drugs. Education and training are most commonly directed at health centre staff and health centres often keep records of patients and prescriptions which can be assessed retrospectively. Observations on the use of drugs in government health facilities are often made by consultants evaluating the implementation of EDPs. These observations are rarely systematic, i.e. they do not include controls, cover only one or two drugs-use indicators and do not relate findings to estimates of drugs needs. In addition, where these observations have been made, they are usually not published and therefore not easily available.

The most commonly used indicators for assessing prescribing practices are average number of drugs per prescription, percentage of prescriptions containing antibiotics and percentage of prescriptions containing an injection. The choice of these indicators has been conditioned by (a) the relative ease with which this data can be collected and (b) the excessive use of antibiotics and injectables. This is because the main problem associated with drugs use relates to over-prescribing. Thus, prescribing is assumed to be more rational if these indicators have lower values.

For example, in ten of the country studies undertaken for the external evaluation of DAP, many variations were reported. In a health centre in *Bangladesh* prescriptions contained an average of 4.1 drugs. In the health centres visited in *Vietnam* prescriptions were only found to list one or two drugs. In *Sudan* 30-60 per cent of prescriptions contained antibiotics (one might expect a more reasonable proportion to be between 10 and 30 per cent) and injections were also reported to be over used. All the country studies showed that there was a lack of training and information on the rational use of drugs and that irrational use was therefore to be expected.

In an evaluation of the EDP in *Mozambique* (MOH Mozambique, 1986), the average number of drugs per prescription was found to be 2.2. In the treatment of diarrhoea 93 per cent of cases were given oral rehydration therapy (ORT) and only 7 per cent anti-diarrhoeal drugs, suggesting that the programme was succeeding in rationalizing drugs use at least for diarrhoeal diseases.

A study evaluating prescribing practices in *Indonesian* health centres (MSH, 1988) pointed to 'a pattern of non-therapeutic prescribing likely to yield inefficient use of drugs resources, maximize development of bacterial resistance, and minimize patient compliance with treatment'. In addition, antibiotics were prescribed more than twice as frequently as ORT for diarrhoeal diseases, one out of four drugs given was an injection and oral or injectable antibiotics were given to 88 per cent of under fives and 65 per cent of patients of five and over. The average number of drugs per case for all diagnoses was 3.8.

In *Angola* a recent evaluation of the drugs programme found that of a total of 539 consultations observed in three provinces, only 12 per cent of patients were judged to have been adequately diagnosed, adequately prescribed for and knew how to take the medicines they had been prescribed (Kanji et al., 1990).

The only published study to have evaluated the impact of an EDP in relation to a 'control area' was carried out in Democratic Yemen (Hogerzeil et al., 1989). This study found that the programme area had an average of 1.5 drugs per prescription, with 47.3 per cent of prescriptions containing an antibiotic and 24.8 per cent containing an injection. The figures for the control area were respectively: 2.4 drugs per prescription, 66.8 per cent prescriptions with antibiotics and 57.8 per cent prescriptions with injections. The difference was found to be significant. However, when comparing the data with estimated needs of injections and antibiotics (based on morbidity data), it was concluded that, despite the impact of the programme in reducing the use of these drugs, antibiotics and injections still appeared to be over used.

Self-medication: A Constraint to the Success of EDPs

One of the main constraints on rational drugs use is the existence of large amounts of drugs not controlled by health workers. Studies from all over the world suggest that a substantial proportion of pharmaceuticals are purchased without a prescription. For example, two independent studies in *India* report that as much as 47 per cent of the drugs in pharmacies in an urban centre in Andhra Pradesh (Krishnaswamy et al., 1985) and an average of 64 per cent in pharmacies in a number of other urban centres in India (Greenhalgh, 1987) were purchased without a doctor's prescription. The first study covered 25,951 drugs, the second 600.

In *Ecuador* a survey of 619 sales of prescription drugs in two urban pharmacies revealed that 51 per cent of the customers presented no prescription (Price, 1989). Many of these 'under the counter drugs', such as chloramphenicol and dipyrone, are potentially hazardous, requiring great care and close monitoring of possible adverse effects to minimize risk. A study of 11,700 drugs sales in the capital of *Ethiopia*, Addis Ababa, found that around 82 per cent were purchased without a prescription. Again, many potentially hazardous drugs were reportedly sold 'under the counter' (Sekhar et al., 1981).

The few studies that have surveyed people's self-medication practices at the community level tend to confirm the findings of the pharmacy surveys, suggesting that self-medication is predominant. Of particular importance are the findings of longitudinal community-based studies in Thailand, the Philippines, Brazil and Ghana. In all these studies families were visited at regular intervals to record the occurrence of common health problems, such as coughs and diarrhoea, and the choice of therapy.

Families in four villages in *Thailand* (Le Grand and Sri Ngernyuang, 1990) were visited at two-weekly intervals during which a total of 1,755 cases of illness were recorded. Of these cases 70 per cent were initially self-treated, half with modern pharmaceuticals and the other half with traditional remedies. In 14 per cent of the cases no treatment was used at all. People consulted health professionals in only 7 per cent of the illness episodes. Around 30 per cent of the pharmaceuticals used were obtained from household stocks. Another 25 per cent came from commercial drugs distribution channels, mostly local grocery shops, but only 9 per cent of the drugs were obtained from the village drugs funds, which were intended to be the main channel for the supply of essential drugs in the Thai PHC programme.

In the *Philippines*, 1,411 episodes of illness were recorded in 126 families in two urban communities (Hardon, 1990). Of these, 92 per cent were treated without consulting a doctor and, again, in approximately half of these cases modern pharmaceuticals were used. This study reported that around 50 per cent of the medications used in the community were obtained from 'informal' sources, including village grocery stores and household stocks.

A comparative urban-rural study in *Ghana* (Wondergem et al., 1989) reported less self-medication in the urban than in the rural communities. In the two rural communities covered, a total of 58 per cent of the cases were self-treated, around half with modern drugs and the other half with herbs. In *Brazil* a household survey in two rural communities (Haak, 1987) reported that 75 per cent of the medications consumed in 188 episodes of illness in both communities were taken without consulting a doctor. The results were the same for both communities, with approximately 30 per cent of the drugs used being on the UN list of banned, withdrawn or severely restricted products.

Apart from pointing out the predominance of self-care, these findings suggest that government health centres are rarely important sources of drugs and that the private and informal sector often account for the bulk of drugs provision. The importance of the household stock and community grocery stores as sources of drugs is apparent in the above case reports from Thailand and the Philippines. EDPs rarely acknowledge the role of informal drugs distribution channels in the delivery of drugs. And, because drugs are often acquired illegally, studies on such channels are rare and difficult to carry out. None the less, the parallel market in Senegal is estimated to be as important, if not more so, than the public sector (Fassin, 1987).

The Irrationality of Diarrhoea Treatment

Because diarrhoea is one of the main killers of children in developing countries and because its fatal consequence can be avoided by timely rehydration, extensive studies have been made of its treatment among children. In addition, campaigns against drugs companies promoting their anti-diarrhoeal drugs have been effective in bringing about changes in many of these companies' marketing practices. The examples below provide an insight into the problem of drugs misuse.

Although it is widely accepted that ORT is the treatment of choice for more than 90 per cent of cases of childhood diarrhoea, studies show that the use (or rather misuse) of drugs is rampant. In *Nigeria*, Isenalumhe and Oviawe (1988) reveal that of 299 children suffering from diarrhoea, 60 per cent were prescribed antibiotics at 77 times the cost of ORT, with an average number of 5.6 drugs prescribed per patient. A household survey in *Indonesia* (Lerman et al., 1988) found that 74 per cent of diarrhoea cases were treated with antibiotics, of which Tetracycline, which is contra-indicated in children, was the most popular. A survey of pharmacists in the *Yemen, Bangladesh and Sri Lanka* showed that, on being presented with a fictitious case of childhood diarrhoea, only 16 of the 75 pharmacists gave the appropriate advice and most recommended drugs (Tomson and Sterky, 1986). The list of studies documenting similar findings is endless. People, even when they are aware of ORT and know how to prepare it, prefer drugs and often injections. The misuse of antibiotics, not only for diarrhoea, but for all coughs and fevers and even also as a 'prevention before a night out' is particularly worrying.

Antibiotic Misuse: Far-reaching Consequences

Officially, in most countries antibiotics are prescription-only drugs. In practice, in most developing countries they are widely available under the counter in many pharmacies, grocery shops and even on street corners. One study of 9,633 over the counter (OTC) orders, i.e. without prescription, revealed that 67 per cent of the orders were for antibiotics (Sekhar et al., 1981). These figures are by no means unusual, in fact they indicate the norm. In a double-edged twist of events, traditional healers, who for years existed on non-allopathic concepts of health and treatment, are reported to be using drugs such as injectable penicillin (Burghart, 1988). Authors have argued that traditional practitioners have taken this step in response to patient demand (Wolffers, 1988; Batia, 1975). Certainly, a practice that combines the traditional and perhaps culturally more acceptable and appropriate health system with the potent injections of allopathic practice, may be attractive to people.

The misuse of antibiotics for diarrhoea or common colds, the pouring of injectable antibiotics onto cuts and wounds and the failure to complete prescribed treatments have created a serious international problem, namely antibiotic resistance. Simply, because chemically bacteria have had enough opportunity to analyse the structures of many of the antibiotics, they have developed complex mechanisms for inactivating or destroying them. Thus, drugs that were highly effective against a host of bacteria only a few decades ago are now almost useless. We are faced with the problem of continually having to produce more powerful antibiotics to treat infections.

Rationality in a Socio-cultural Perspective

WHO's concept of rational drugs use is mainly defined in medical and financial terms. But people have their own rationales for deciding on therapies. Irrationality, defined from a medical point of view, may be totally rational from the consumer's point of view. 'Hot-cold' beliefs concerning the cause of an illness often determine the choice of therapy. In 'cold' disorders 'cold' therapies are often avoided even though the health professional may consider them essential. For example, the Mende people of Sierra Leone consider pharmaceuticals too powerful for children, herbal medicines good for restoring the balance of the body, tablets weaker than injections, a red coloured drug useful for replacing or purifying blood, bitter tasting drugs helpful in expelling heat from the body and purgatives useful for inducing abortions because they 'cut' the womb (Bledsoe and Goubaud, 1985 and 1988). In the Philippines a drug may be considered not useful if it is not *hiyang* (suitable) for the patient (Hardon, 1987), or in India because the patient has no *abhiyasa* (compatibility) with that medicine (Nichter, 1980).

The same drug may well be effective for another person, indicating that people relate efficacy to an interaction between the chemical component of the drug and an individual's constitution.

People's economic conditions also play an important part in affecting the use of drugs. From the consumer's point of view, the potential adverse effects of irrational use may be irrelevant in the harsh context of his or her daily life. For example, if a drug is said to be good for certain ailments and is easily available through informal distribution channels, many poor people will use it in the hope that they will be able to continue working and thus avoid losing a day's wages and/or production. A small farmer who has a fever cannot afford to follow the 'rational' medical advice to go home and rest. He or she is obliged to take antipyretics to continue working. Similarly, if a drug treatment has been effective before and there are still some tablets left over, then it also makes sense to keep these tablets for the next time round. Both money and time can thus be saved.

Have 15 Years of Essential Drugs Achieved Anything?

Given the rampant misuse of drugs, why is there so much emphasis on increasing the supply of essential drugs? Why has training on rational use lagged so far behind? A pessimist could conclude that in the current situation DAP's overall impact is very limited for, where essential drugs are available, they are likely to be misused.

Part of the reason for the supply bias seems to lie in the politics surrounding the formulation and implementation of essential drugs policies. The foregoing chapters show that governments have to deal with powerful interest groups, of which the pharmaceutical industry and organized physicians are the most important. In many developing countries both groups oppose the essential drugs concept for reasons that have been outlined. To them, increasing the supply of essential drugs in the public sector is less threatening than informing health workers and the general public (the two main target audiences in this field) on the rational use of drugs. An informed public is much more of a threat to pharmaceutical sales than a 'parallel drugs supply' that caters to the poorest, who cannot afford the private sector anyway.

There are, however, more reasons why the programmes have had only a limited impact on the rational use of drugs. We have seen that in using drugs people do not necessarily rely on the advice of health workers and that informal and private distribution channels are important sources of drugs. In other words, much of the use and distribution of drugs in developing countries happens outside the control of government health professionals. Training and education programmes are regarded as being exclusively for the benefit of the poor who rely on the formal public health sector. Of course, the situation differs from country to country. A country like Mozambique, for example, has a very small private sector and people do rely on the public health care system for their drugs. Generally, however, the failure of policy-makers at national and international levels to pay attention to private and informal drugs distribution channels is serious, as are the consequences of this neglect.

Finally, the socio-cultural context plays a part in determining how, when and which drugs are used for which ailments. This socio-cultural reinterpretation of 'rational drugs use' is probably the most difficult to counteract. People take drugs according to their own ideas of safety and efficacy. They also make their own cost-benefit analysis based on their own living conditions. This 'reinterpreted' rationality is rarely acknowledged in policy formulation and implementation.

The picture, however, is not entirely gloomy. Even though DAP's achievements have failed to live up to the expectations of all those concerned, much has changed in the world's drugs situation because of the existence of DAP and the consistent political, economic and technical assistance WHO has provided to member states. At a time when both the supply of drugs and information about them was being controlled by Western multinationals, WHO managed to bring the supply, cost, dumping and use of drugs onto the international policy agenda. Implicit in its philosophy was the belief that health and, consequently, access to essential drugs was a human right. This was a courageous stance in the face of the many powerful vested interests that felt threatened by the possibility of having their profits curtailed. As the preceding chapters show, in keeping a dialogue open without losing its resolve, WHO's leadership handled the real and potential conflict between the various factions with consummate skill.

On a political level, Dr Mahler's speech to the World Health Assembly (WHA) in 1975 brought the drugs issue onto the international policy agenda. Through his analysis of the myriad of unethical and sometimes illegal practices in the sale and distribution of drugs in developing countries, he not only created an environment for attempting to change the existing situation, but also assured political and technical support to member states that were willing to rationalize their drugs systems. The publication of a model list of essential drugs in 1977 provided not only the technical basis but also the inspirational and moral support for Bangladesh's new drugs policy. In Kenya the list became the basis for thinking about drugs policies and, for Mozambique, it provided a validation for the policies it was already pursuing. More importantly, perhaps, in taking up the drugs issue and setting up DAP, WHO indirectly confronted the multinationals' self-professed monopoly on knowledge and information about the procurement, marketing, distribution, efficacy, use and adverse effects of drugs. In doing this it challenged the ideas and norms that perpetuated the multinationals' power and monopoly. The pharmaceutical industry was forced onto the defensive to the extent that, in an attempt to pre-empt WHO's drawing up of an ethical code on marketing drugs, it introduced its own code, albeit a voluntary and toothless one. None the less, before this such an event would have been unthinkable. Some companies have now taken a serious look at the moral and ethical issues surrounding marketing and progress has been made in this area.

In its support for the essential drugs concept, WHO created an environment for change and provided a forum in which consumer groups could affect the policy process. These groups began to monitor the activities of the pharmaceutical industry during the 1970s and set up an international network to act as a countervailing force to the multinational corporations. The creation of an administrative unit for the action programme in 1981 formalized WHO's responsibility and operational involvement in the drugs field. This in turn helped Health Action International (HAI), a coalition of consumer, professional and development action groups from 27 countries, to hold its inaugural meeting in Geneva in 1982. The existence of the action programme gave HAI an international body that could be lobbied and pushed into adopting more stringent measures against the industry's unethical practices.

Moreover, by the mid to late 1980s, WHO's advocacy of the essential drugs concept had led to various international agencies, governments, professional bodies and NGOs accepting and advocating the concept. The UN High Commission on Refugees introduced essential drugs into refugee camps. In 1986 the European Parliament adopted a resolution stating that pharmaceutical exports should focus on essential drugs and, in 1989, the Overseas Development Agency (UK) adopted an essential drugs policy for pharmaceutical aid. The British Medical Association, the Commonwealth Pharmaceutical Association and the International Federation of Pharmacists are just a few examples of professional bodies that have adopted the essential drugs concept. NGOs such as the Christian Medical Commission, OXFAM, *Médecins sans Frontières* and *Frères des Hommes* have actively campaigned for the concept (LSHTM/KIT, 1989).

WHO's involvement in assessing different countries' drugs situations and making recommendations on how to improve them was often instrumental in mobilizing donor agencies to support drugs programmes financially. Though seldom achieving national drugs policies, WHO did provide 'seed money' with which to initiate the process and, even if all aspects were not tackled, change did occur and often for the good. Examples were set to show what governments could achieve if they had the political will. Democratic Yemen, for example, was an excellent case of the sensible use of WHO funds through investing in the development of human resources. In addition to bilateral and multilateral agreements between donor and recipient countries for funding EDPs, almost 70 per cent of DAP's US$22.3 million proposed budget for 1988/9 was destined for country support activities (LSHTM/KIT, 1989).

Technical support to developing countries also played an important role. This was provided either through consultants (DAP staff or independents), fellowships for developing countries' personnel, or guidelines and training manuals on subjects ranging from how to quantify drugs needs to how to develop drugs policies. Furthermore, DAP organized and sponsored a host of national, regional and international workshops on subjects related to the essential drugs concept, which brought together people working on similar issues and in search of practical solutions. The 1989 evaluation of DAP (LSHTM/KIT, 1989) made the following statement about the technical materials produced by the programme:

> However, questions do arise about why certain publications produced years ago still remain drafts. For example, the revised curricula for medical faculties have not been published. Material on patent rights exercised by industry, rational prescribing, compliance and public education as well as the question of the private sector and national drugs policies is either little developed or absent. In addition, requests for provision of information for prescribers and consumers appear to have been dropped.... These topics would almost certainly have aggravated tensions with industry and were perhaps left alone for that reason.

The above observation is indicative of the kind of balancing act required of and performed by WHO in its attempt to take on a highly political and economic issue while remaining within its mandate of being a technical organization providing technical information to member states.

In concluding WHO's achievements in the field of essential drugs, three points need to be borne in mind. The first is that WHO is a technical agency with a mandate to provide technical information and support to member states. It is therefore to the credit of its former leadership that health came to be defined as a development issue and attempts to influence change moved into the political, economic and social arenas. The drugs debate is an excellent example of the many issues involved. None the less, throughout Dr Mahler's term as director-general, tensions existed within the organization and between it and others about the role of WHO. Proponents of the 'technical role', who argued that WHO should only provide technical expertise and information and should leave policy decisions to member states, were missing or avoiding the point. The use of technology and the dissemination of information is rarely neutral. Mahler never advocated interfering in national policy-making, but he encouraged member states to adopt policies that arose out of a concern for social equity, even when it was against the national élite's interests to implement such policies. It was this encouragement, together with WHO's public support of equity, that incurred the wrath of the opposition.

Secondly, WHO has to rely for its existence on funds provided by its member states and the bulk of these come from the US, Western Europe and Japan. Of the top 25 pharmaceutical companies in terms of sales in 1988, 12 were American, three German, four British, three Swiss, two Japanese and one French, with a total sales value in 1988 of almost US$67,500 million (Chetley, 1990). There is an obvious conflict of interests. With multinational drugs companies regularly lobbying their home governments to promote their business interests at home and abroad, government departments will naturally come into conflict with each other in pursuing their aims. For example, the interests of the Department of Trade in promoting the domestic pharmaceutical industry are bound to clash with those of the

Department of Health in pursuing a rational drugs policy. Governments deal with such conflicts in very different ways. Whereas the Europeans are less confrontational and more open to dialogue in their dealings with WHO, the US takes a much stronger position and, in 1986, allegedly because of its dissatisfaction with the Nairobi Conference on Rational Drugs the previous year (LSHTM/KIT, 1989), refused to pay its assessed contribution of 25 per cent to the organization. In terms of support for DAP, the US contributed nothing towards the US$31.5 million for global and interregional activities from 1980 to 1989 and neither did West Germany. Britain gave US$1.9 million, Switzerland US$1.3 million, Japan US$175,000 and France US$542,000. The bulk of DAP's extra-budgetary funds, which were essential for carrying out its work, came from The Netherlands and Denmark (WHO/APED, 1989).

Thirdly, according to its mandate WHO can only respond to requests made by member states and can impose neither itself nor its policies upon them. Whereas at the WHAs most developing countries were willing to vote for resolutions in support of the essential drugs concept, their willingness to implement national policies at home was less enthusiastic. The sorts of pressures brought to bear on countries attempting change have been described in other chapters; if WHO was under considerable pressure to dilute the content and advocacy of the concept, the pressure on national governments was even more forceful. In the absence of government will WHO can do little other than exchange and disseminate information on positive examples.

Given this context, WHO, mainly through the political adroitness of Dr Mahler and his policy adviser, Dr Cohen, achieved much. In health and development circles 'essential drugs' has become an accepted concept against which few would argue. The number of countries with EDLs and programmes *has* increased dramatically since about 1984. Essential drugs have become more available for primary level services in many countries and the rational use of drugs has been identified and quantified as an important issue. National drugs policies have been brought to the fore of health debates. Fortunately, the industry has been forced to examine its marketing practices and, even though there is a long way to go, some companies have begun to put their houses in order.

References

Batia, J.C. (1975) 'Traditional healers and modern medicine'. *Social Science and Medicine*, 9, 15-21

Bledsoe, C.H. and M. Goubaud (1985) 'The reinterpretation of Western pharmaceuticals among the Mende of Sierra Leone'. *Social Science and Medicine*, 21 (3), 275-82

————— (1988) 'The reinterpretation and distribution of Western pharmaceuticals: An example of the Mende of Sierra Leone'. In Geest and Whyte (eds), q.v., 253-77

Burghart, R. (1988) 'Penicillin: An ancient Ayurvedic medicine'. In Geest and Whyte (eds), q.v., 289-99

Chetley, A. (1990) *A healthy business? World health and the pharmaceutical industry*. London: Zed Books

Fassin, D. (1987) 'The illicit sale of pharmaceuticals in Africa: Sellers and clients in the suburbs of Dakar'. *Tropical and Geographical Medicine*, November, 166-70

Geest, S.v.d. and S.R. Whyte (eds) (1988) *The context of medicines in developing countries. Studies in pharmaceutical anthropology*. Dordrecht: Kluwer Academic Publishers

Greenhalgh, T. (1987) 'Drug prescription and self-medication in India: An exploratory survey'. *Social Science and Medicine*, 25 (3), 307-18

Haak, H. (1987) 'Pharmaceuticals in two Brazilian villages: Lay practices and perceptions'. *Social Science and Medicine*, 27 (12), 1415-27

Hardon, A. (1987) 'The use of modern pharmaceuticals in a Filipino village: Doctors' prescriptions and self-medication'. *Social Science and Medicine*, 25 (3), 277-92

————— (1990) 'Confronting ill health: Medicines, self-care and the poor in Manila'. Unpublished Ph.D thesis, University of Amsterdam

Hogerzeil, H., G. Walker, A. Sallami and G. Fernando (1989) 'Impact of an essential drugs programme on availability and rational use of drugs'. *The Lancet*, January, 141-2

Isenalumhe, A. and O. Oviawe (1988) 'Polypharmacy: Its cost burden and barrier to medical care in a drug-oriented health care system'. *International Journal of Health Services*, 18 (2), 335-42

Islam, N., J. Martinussen and S. Rifkin (1989) 'Evaluation of WHO's APED'. *Bangladesh Case Study*, London: LSHTM/KIT

Kanji, N., G. Munishi and G. Sterky (1989) 'Evaluation of WHO's APED'. *Tanzania Case Study*, London: LSHTM/KIT

Kanji, N., M. Bjorck, E. M'Finda, P. Mayembe, M.J. Soares and S. N'kuku (1990) *Evaluation of the essential drugs programme in the People's Republic of Angola*. Luanda: MOH

Krishnaswamy, K., D. Kumar and G. Radhaiah (1985) 'A drug survey: Precepts and practices'. *European Journal of Clinical Pharmacology*, 29 (3), 363-70

Le Grande, A. and L. Sri Ngernyuang (1989) *Herbal drugs in primary health care, Thailand: The impact of promotional activities on drug consumption, provision and self-reliance*. Amsterdam: Royal Tropical Institute

Lerman, S., D. Shepard and R. Cash (1985) 'Treatment of diarrhoea in Indonesian children: What it costs and who pays for it'. *The Lancet*, 21 (II), 651-4

LSHTM/KIT (1989) *An evaluation of WHO's Action Programme on Essential Drugs*. London: LSHTM/KIT

Lunde, P., C. Matai and M. Mamdani (1989) 'An evaluation of WHO's APED'. *Kenya Case Study*. London: LSHTM/KIT

MOH Mozambique (1986) *Evaluation of the Essential Drugs Programme.* Maputo: MOH

MSH (1988) *Where does the Tetracycline go?* Boston: Management Sciences for Health

Nichter, M. (1980) 'The lay person's perception of medicine as a way of looking at the utilization of multiple therapy systems in the Indian context'. *Social Science and Medicine*, 14B, 225-33

Price, L. (1989) 'In the shadow of biomedicine: Self-medication in two Ecuadorian pharmacies'. *Social Science and Medicine*, 28 (9), 905-15

Sekhar, C., R. Raina and G. Pillai (1981) 'Some aspects of drug use in Ethiopia'. *Tropical Doctor*, 11, 116-18

Tomson, G. and G. Sterky (1986) 'Self-prescribing with the aid of pharmacies in three Asian developing countries'. *The Lancet*, 13, 620-2

UNICEF (1988) 'UNICEF's Supply Function'. Mimeo, New York: UNICEF Supply Division

WHO/APED (1989) *Progress report on the Action Programme on Essential Drugs.* May, Geneva: WHO

Wolffers, I. (1988) 'De rol van geneesmidelen in een geisoleerd gebied (Centraal Kalimantan)'. *Pharmaceutisch Weekblad*, 123, 510-14

Wondergem, P., K. Senah and E. Glover (1989) 'Herbal drugs in primary health care'. Unpublished paper for an assessment of the relevance of herbal drugs in PHC and some suggestions for strengthening PHC, Ghana

6

New Horizons in the 1990s

Anita Hardon and Najmi Kanji

Whereas in the 1980s the Action Programme on Essential Drugs (APED) was a global concerted effort, in the 1990s new factors are affecting WHO's coordinating role and challenging the original policy framework and plan of action. In this chapter we discuss four interrelated trends which have a bearing on the future direction of the programme: WHO's diminishing leadership and advocacy role; the emphasis on pharmaceutical cost-recovery as a component of structural adjustment programmes; the increased attention being paid to the rational use of drugs; and an increased demand for drugs related to the AIDS epidemic. Two further important issues are also dealt with, namely the feasibility of expanding the essential drugs concept to the field of contraceptive methods and the role of industry in the provision and use of drugs.

The Leadership Role of WHO Diminishes

At the 1988 WHA Dr Halfden Mahler officially retired and Dr Hiroshi Nakajima was elected as the new director-general of WHO. Much rumour surrounds the election of Dr Nakajima, but, as is the nature of such happenings, little of the background and politicking around the election is documented. Some people suggested that many votes were bought through the promise of Japanese aid money, while others were convinced that the new director-general best suited the needs of the organization, whose responsibility it was to provide technical information rather that actively advocate policy. An editorial in *The Lancet* stated that Dr Nakajima might emphasize technology much more and asked if this would happen at the expense of policy. In relation to the drugs companies, the editorial (SCRIP, 1988a) went on to say that whereas 'he will [not] do what industry wants, but the industry is likely to receive a more favourable reception'. Interestingly enough, at the very assembly that elected Dr Nakajima, the US announced that, to cover some of its arrears in payments to WHO, it was making a contribution of $20.5 million. The gesture was interpreted by many as support for the policies that Nakajima was representing (Chetley, 1990).

The changes in DAP following Nakajima's election generated considerable doubt and concern about WHO's capacity to take a leadership role in promoting the essential drugs concept. As donors watched DAP's operations they began to look around for other ways of supporting and promoting essential drugs policies and programmes.

Many of DAP's problems had to do with the resignation of the programme manager and the programme's move from the Director-Generals Office to the new Drug Policies and Management (DPM) division, to which in 1990 the former head of the Pharmaceuticals (PHA) division, was appointed as director. As Chapter 2 shows, the relationship between the PHA and DAP had long been tense and the creation of a new division did not resolve the dispute between the two units. DAP's programme manager, Dr Antezana, remained in control of DAP's budget and operations.

In an apparent attempt to regain the initiative in the field of drugs after three years of policy drift and demoralization among most of the programme staff, in early 1991 DAP presented its Management Advisory Committee with a DAP/WHO African initiative. As we have seen, DAP supported successful essential drugs programmes in African countries, but, partly because of problems between WHO's Africa Regional Office (AFRO) and DAP in Geneva, there had been a lack of systematic regional planning. The new programme aimed to decentralize DAP support to the region through three sub-regional offices, to strengthen the technical and managerial capacity of the African region and to strengthen the quality of PHC by enhancing community participation (DAP/WHO, 1991).

While DAP's donors welcomed the focus on Africa, they felt that the plan was insufficiently developed to justify the large amounts of funds requested. Furthermore, they asked for better coordination with UNICEF and AFRO, particularly with respect to the implementation of the Bamako Initiative (Hodgkin, 1991).

In many ways the discussions about the African initiative reflected DAP's diminishing leadership role. While in the 1980s donors had supported virtually anything the programme director suggested (even if the plans were not developed in much detail), in the early 1990s they started to question DAP's capability and role in this field. Further discussion on the expansion of activities to the African region was planned for the 1992 Management Advisory Committee meeting and, for the 1992/3 biennium, a budget of approximately US$24 million has been approved, which is similar to that of the preceding biennium (Essential Drugs Monitor, 1991).

In launching the Bamako Initiative UNICEF appears to have established itself as an important, in fact powerful, actor in the field of essential drugs. Unlike WHO's, its country offices are involved in the actual implementation of health programmes, have played a very active role in promoting immunization, oral rehydration and breast feeding and are now developing the Bamako Initiative further. UNICEF's country offices have access to large amounts of money for health programmes. The DAP budget of around US$20 million for a two-year planning period is comparable to that of one UNICEF country office. Furthermore, UNICEF is increasingly coordinating with the World Bank, which in the late 1980s and early 1990s increased its presence dramatically in sub-Saharan Africa. Nigeria, Cameroon, Ghana, Madagascar and Togo are all countries in which UNICEF and the World Bank are cooperating. The World Bank/UNICEF partnership clearly has a much greater financial capacity to effect drugs programmes in developing countries than WHO ever had.

The support mechanisms and emphases on implementation and policy formulation of the World Bank and UNICEF differ in a number of ways from those developed by DAP in the 1980s. For a start, DAP adopted a very flexible approach towards developing national drugs policies, in which much depended on the initiative of the country in question. In other words, whatever they proposed was used as an entry point. In some countries the first step was to strengthen the drugs regulatory authorities and develop an essential drugs list. In others the initial involvement was in a regional essential drugs programme, with national level policy following at a later stage. UNICEF is more actively involved in policy implementation at the country level and tends to follow a more top-down approach.

These differences in involvement at the country level are related to differences in the nature of the organizations. WHO is a specialized UN agency funded by mandatory and voluntary contributions from its member states and from the United Nations Development Programme (UNDP) (Williams, 1987). UNICEF is also part of the UN, but apart from its multi-lateral funds, it raises extra money through the sale of Christmas cards and other fund-raising activities which account for approximately a quarter of its total budget (UNICEF, 1990). UNICEF is in fact the only UN agency to receive money directly from the public. It has a strong field presence in developing countries, whereas WHO's structure at the country level is very weak.

Because UNICEF does not rely solely on donor governments it can develop its own policies and strategies. In promoting child survival it has always combined advocacy with giving technical advice. Furthermore, it is free to work with governments and NGOs, whereas WHO usually has to work through the Ministry of Health of the country in question.

The World Bank, which is also registered as a specialized UN agency, is primarily involved in financing development projects. The management of the bank is not answerable to the UN, but to its own board of governors consisting of the finance ministers of 155 member countries (Hancock, 1989). The Ministry of Finance is its counterpart in a given country, apart from any other ministry that happens to be involved in a particular development project.

With respect to the work of the agencies in the field of essential drugs, WHO currently has more technical expertise than UNICEF and the World Bank. In the 1980s DAP staff gained considerable experience in supporting countries to develop the various components of essential drugs programmes and policies. The World Bank and UNICEF still lack such expertise. Though they have made efforts to strengthen essential drugs units, these can in no way take over DAP's function in this field. As mentioned, in some cases assistance is requested from DAP, but there also appears to be a trend towards tapping the expertise of private consultancy agencies. Now that DAP's capacity to act is diminishing and the developing countries still lack the required know-how and resources, these US- and European-based consultancy agencies see a new market emerging for essential drugs expertise.

Though ensuring the technical support required in the short term, the increased role of private consultants in this field may in the long term weaken some of DAP's core functions. The main problem is that the transfer of knowledge and expertise to people in developing countries is unlikely to be an important function of these agencies. Nor are they likely to be effective advocates of the essential drugs concept.

Pharmaceutical Cost Recovery and Structural Adjustment

With the implementation of structural adjustment programmes in many developing countries in the 1980s, health budgets (which were already limited) often decreased in real terms. At the same time, demands on health services increased because of high population growth rates, low-intensity warfare, famines, refugee problems and the AIDS epidemic. The effects of cuts in the social sectors are all too apparent. According to the 1990 *Human Development Report* (UNDP, 1991: 18): 'Many countries recorded major reverses in human progress, with rising rates of child malnutrition and infant mortality, particularly in sub-Saharan Africa and Latin America.' Worldwide the report estimates that 1,500 million people still lack access to primary health care (PHC), which in many countries means that they lack access to essential drugs and rely on the private sector for their pharmaceutical needs.

The central tenet of structural adjustment policies is that growth can be achieved only through an export-led economy within which the private sector is given every opportunity and facility to promote production. The state is seen as inherently inefficient and its role in the social services is reduced. The reward for accepting and implementing measures to promote this ideology is a flow of loans and aid to the country concerned, but more often than not this money goes towards servicing the debt rather than developing the country. These policies have not achieved the stated objectives of promoting growth, but they have managed to reverse the net flow of capital from the rich countries to the poor (Kanji et al., 1991).

In its 1990 poverty report, the World Bank (1991) promotes the provision of basic social services (with PHC, family planning, nutrition and primary education mentioned specifically) as an essential strategy for alleviating poverty. The provision of basic health services under tight budget constraints should be achieved, according to the World Bank, by shifting the allocation of funds from higher level health services to the more basic ones (thereby serving both equity and efficiency objectives) and by introducing fees for those who can afford them. The public sector should complement the private sector which, according to the World Bank, is primarily responsible for curative health care.

Worried about prevailing economic conditions and the dire state of PHC services in sub-Saharan Africa and elsewhere, in an address to African ministers of health in September 1987 UNICEF's executive director proposed the following solution. Drugs provided by donors and international agencies would be sold to communities at marked-up prices. The money thus raised would be used for strengthening primary level mother and child health care programmes and for paying health workers' salaries. This idea was what came to be known as the Bamako Initiative (UNICEF, 1988). The Bamako Initiative accepts that a proportion of the community is too poor to pay and suggests that this group should be exempted. Mechanisms and criteria for exemption are, however, simplistic and fail to reflect the complex power relationships that exist at the local levels of health care. The scheme assumes that because people had always paid traditional healers high prices for scarce drugs, this 'willingness' to pay actually reflected their ability to pay. Critics stress that, as health workers' salaries were also dependent on the amount of money collected through drugs sales, there would be an obvious incentive to over-prescribe and promote irrational drugs use (Chabot, 1988; Kanji, 1989). Similarly, questions are raised about how collecting local currency would solve the problem of buying drugs that had to be imported with convertible currency. UNICEF is also said to have underestimated the seriousness of problems related to management capabilities, decision-making and accounting at the local level and to have held an over optimistic view of what local communities were potentially capable of achieving (UNICEF/HAI/OXFAM, 1990).

Although recent documents on the Bamako Initiative attempt to deal with some of the above concerns, it is difficult to define clearly what the scheme now is. It seems that, at present, as long as the three components of community financing, community participation and essential drugs are covered, the Bamako Initiative can be taken to mean almost anything related to strengthening basic health services (UNICEF, 1990).

According to the 1991 Bamako Initiative Progress Report to UNICEF's Executive Board (UNICEF, 1991), most countries in Africa have begun to implement 'Bamako-type' projects, having moved through various stages of assessment, analysis and action planning. A core group of 12 countries has reached a clear definition of the initiative and UNICEF has created a Bamako Initiative Development Fund of around US$20 million, which is about half DAP's annual budget. In Benin, for example, the Bamako Initiative is integrated into the National Health Strategy. Virtually all community health centres are reportedly implementing the initiative, with around 50 per cent receiving UNICEF support. Pharmaceutical cost recovery is the core component. The Bamako Initiative also covers about half the health centres in Guinea, with a cost recovery system based on the collection of fees for drugs. In Burundi, the costs are recovered through an insurance system, whereby people buy a *Carte Assurance Medical* each year in exchange for free services in the public health centres. Coverage of this scheme is reportedly low.

Thus, the implementation of structural adjustment programmes and the realization that these have serious health consequences have resulted in increased attempts to find measures to enhance the efficiency and coverage of public health care. Expanding the distribution of essential drugs programmes and introducing a fee-paying system are seen as important solutions to these problems by many international and national health policy-makers. These developments have made drugs financing a central issue in essential drugs programmes, especially in sub-Saharan Africa. This is a challenge to DAP because drugs financing was not a part of either its original framework or its revised drugs strategy. It remains to be seen how this trend towards pharmaceutical cost recovery will affect the rational use of drugs.

The Rational Use of Drugs: Focus for the 1990s

The 1985 Nairobi conference laid the basis for the revised drugs strategy, the main aim of which was to enhance the rational use of drugs. WHO's focus on the *rational use of drugs* developed in response to the realization that the simple availability of drugs does not always solve the problem of drugs use. This realization led to the reorientation of the debate within DAP away from questions of pure logistics and supply to a consideration of what happens when drugs are made available.

In line with revised drugs strategies, methods to improve prescribing and self-medication practices are increasingly being introduced into governmental and non-governmental essential drugs programmes. Such interventions usually take the form of producing manuals for health workers and training them for different levels of health care. More recently DAP has started to encourage governments to develop comprehensive 'information, education and communications' plans. Such plans have been developed for Nigeria and Malawi (Remstrad, 1987; DAP/WHO, 1990) and are likely to become models for many other countries intending to rationalize drugs use.

As we saw in Chapter 5, the success of many of these interventions has not yet been assessed and, as a consequence, their impact is not yet known, neither can any sound advice be given on which types of interventions are most promising. DAP will need to do a lot more work before seeing a real improvement in the rational use of drugs, but in so doing is likely to be constrained by governments less interested in enhancing rational use than in supplying the essential drugs. In supplying drugs governments can gain politically, for people get the impression that the government is helping them. Enhancing rational drugs use is a far less rewarding activity. People are not waiting for health workers to tell them that they are taking their drugs incorrectly.

It is in the field of rational drugs use that NGOs such as HAI, the Christian Medical Association, and the International Network for the Rational Use of Drugs (INRUD) are likely to play a crucial role. More than governments and WHO, these NGOs direct interventions towards consumers and the general public.

Whereas in the 1970s it was mostly consumer and health NGOs from developed countries that were concerned about the malpractices involved in the distribution and use of pharmaceuticals, in the 1980s there was a rapid increase in the involvement of third world NGOs. Many countries now have research and documentation centres through which to provide interested health professionals, consumers and government institutions with up to date information on the safety and efficacy of drugs. Examples of such institutions are Health Action Information Network (HAIN) in the Philippines, and the Drug Information and Action Centre (DIAC) in Thailand. In addition, researchers and teachers from academic institutions are becoming involved. They increasingly see the need to change the medical curriculum to include the essential drugs concept and to engage in research projects to monitor prescribing practices in different health care facilities.

NGOs are also involved in integrating the essential drugs concept into PHC at the grass-roots level. Such community-based health programmes are developing innovative ways of helping people in the villages and slums of underdeveloped countries learn to use medicines more wisely and to understand their possible risks and benefits. Methods have been developed that promote critical thinking as well as awareness of contradictions and conflicts of interest, reflecting an empowering approach to community health education. The social marketing approach, advocated by agencies such as UNICEF, is regarded as too manipulative in that it attempts to 'sell' appropriate health care in much the same way as pharmaceutical industries sell their products.

In working at the grass-roots level it becomes obvious that change towards a more rational use of pharmaceuticals will be impossible so long as the environment in which people take drugs remains so irrational (Hardon, 1991; Lopez and Kroeger, 1990). People receive 'irrational' messages over the radio, from doctors' prescribing patterns and at the various pharmacies and other outlets where they can buy drugs over the counter without a prescription. They are confronted with conflicting messages and tend to continue to use drugs in the manner in which, in their perceptions and from their experiences, they have worked best. Education on the proper use of medicines has a limited effect if the existing drugs distribution patterns and information sources are not rationalized.

From working at the grass roots it also becomes clear that 'rational drugs use' cannot be defined with the universal criteria of safety, efficacy, affordability and need. Health workers who try to change patterns of drug use realize more and more that what is rational depends very much on what people think is rational, what their living conditions are and on what drugs and diagnostic tools are available in the health care context. Medically speaking, analgesics are not, for example, needed to treat a headache. Rest is also an effective treatment. However, if a labourer needs to work and his headache is preventing him from doing so, then the analgesic can be considered necessary for economic reasons. The analgesic costs 20 cents, not working would cost US$10. Thus, the criteria should be related to the reality in which people live.

Likewise, in a well equipped health care setting it would be irrational to prescribe an anti-malarial drug to a patient with a fever of unknown origin. However, if health care workers lack the diagnostic tools with which to test if patients have malaria, then such a prescription may well be considered rational. They may not know for certain if a patient actually has malaria, but do know that many patients suffer malaria in the area. In this health care context the benefits of giving an anti-malarial are likely to outweigh the risks.

This contextualizing of the 'rational drugs use' concept is a major challenge to DAP. It implies that criteria for 'rationality' cannot be defined at the national level and then applied at the district and local levels of health care. It emphasizes the need for a 'bottom-up' approach and community participation, and methods that are advocated for health education in the context of PHC. It requires dialogue between pharmacological experts, health workers and consumers. Indeed it requires essential drugs programmes to be integrated more into PHC, more than has been the case to date.

AIDS and Increasing Demands for Drugs

The AIDS epidemic poses a serious health threat to all countries, but particularly to developing countries without a health care infrastructure and with a high incidence of infection. The most affected areas at present are located in much of central, eastern and southern Africa and a number of Caribbean countries. In its infancy the epidemic has already induced a sharp increase in the rate of tuberculosis and other infectious diseases in a group of primarily young adults who were not previously ill. The epidemic affects the health care system drastically, costing hospital beds, staff time and drugs for the extended period in which the patients require health care. Drugs have an important role to play in the care of HIV-positive patients. According to Foster (1991), essential drugs can cope adequately with many of the early infections and a number of symptoms and can provide much relief and comfort. In Uganda, for example, nine relatively inexpensive drugs plus anti-tuberculosis therapy have been shown to provide a high degree of relief for AIDS patients. These drugs are co-trimoxazole, metronidazole, ketoconazole, chlorpromazine, chloroquine, aspirin or paracetamol, codeine, calamine lotion and petroleum jelly (Katabira and Goodgame, 1989). Thus, to confront the AIDS epidemic, essential drugs programmes will need to distribute more drugs, which will mean not only an additional financial burden on the programmes but also, as the epidemic develops, extra skilled staff at the basic level of health services to deal with the constant monitoring of these patients and their changing drugs requirements. According to one multi-country study (Over et al., 1988), estimates of costs for a lifetime's treatment range from US$132 to US$1,585 in Zaire and US$104 to US$631 in Tanzania. These figures include costs incurred by the family as well as by the health services. The costs of treatment are generally higher when the AIDS patient also suffers from tuberculosis. A hospital-based study in Zambia (Chela et al., 1989) found that HIV-positive patients without tuberculosis paid an average of US$24 for drugs treatment during their stay in hospital, while HIV-positive patients with tuberculosis paid US$33. In comparison, HIV-negative patients without tuberculosis paid an average of US$8 for drugs treatment during their stay.

In that it affects young people, the epidemic is likely to diminish family income and thus the capacity to pay user fees. This will impose a special constraint on Bamako Initiative programmes, which rely on user fees. HIV-positive patients are likely to need more drugs than others but be in a worse position to pay. In areas where the incidence of AIDS is high, this loss of income to the programmes can be considerable and lead to a substantial decrease in the amount of revenue raised.

Apart from curative care, the AIDS epidemic also calls for preventive approaches and the distribution of condoms, which are usually not included in the list of drugs supplied by essential drugs programmes. It is essential to keep the cost of condoms as low as possible to enhance their accessibility, in contrast to the private sector where they are usually too expensive for the poor. Including condoms in drugs kits appears to be an inevitable consequence of the AIDS epidemic. This seems to introduce an argument in favour of the more systematic inclusion of other contraceptives as well, thus changing the scope of the essential drugs programmes and requiring closer coordination with family planning services.

The Rational Use of Contraceptives: Free Choice?

It is remarkable that to date WHO and other agencies involved in this field have not applied the essential drugs concept to contraceptives, while technically speaking the most commonly used methods (hormonal pills, injections, implants and IUDs) are pharmaceuticals. The cause of this is most probably the fact that at the national level contraceptives have been distributed through family planning programmes, funded by donors other than the essential drugs programmes.

Questions of safety in relation to contraceptives started to emerge in the 1980s and, more recently, women and health groups have been calling for the criteria of safety, efficacy, affordability and medical need to be applied to contraceptives as well (Hardon, 1990). As with essential drugs, people involved in family planning programmes are realizing that the focus on supply has limited the programmes' effectiveness. More attention needs to be paid to the quality of family planning programmes to ensure that the contraceptives are used properly, but also (and this is different from what has been called for in the field of essential drugs) to ensure that people have a *free choice* from a range of different contraceptives (UNFPA, 1991).

Central to the essential drugs concept is the idea that the number of different therapeutic options should be reduced to the safest, most effective and cheapest. Policy-makers involved in implementing family planning programmes are increasingly advocating a 'cafeteria' approach in which people are offered a maximum range of options. It is argued that the balance of safety and efficacy can differ from one method to another, as do other attributes of the method such as the duration of efficacy (ranging from one day to five years), the mode of administration (oral, injection, insertion in the arm) and the reversibility. People's needs are seen to differ depending on the number of children they still want and the level of efficacy that is appropriate (Bruce, 1989).

This difference in orientation of the policies involved limits the feasibility of incorporating contraceptives into essential drugs programmes. On the other hand, the concept of choice, as applied to contraceptives, has always been a challenge to the essential drugs concept. It is precisely this argument that doctors have used to oppose the concept, claiming that they need the freedom to choose the method that best fits their patients. Once people are given the opportunity to participate in defining rational drugs use in the context of PHC programmes, they too may call for the retention of some drugs, because these fit their personal needs.

The issue of choice will constantly confront people involved in the implementation of essential drugs programmes, especially when community participation is strengthened and, accordingly, lay people and local health workers are consulted more systematically than in the past. Against this background, increasing the scope of essential drugs programmes to that of ensuring the accessibility and rational use of pharmaceuticals *and* contraceptives should be seen as an additional challenge to DAP's framework, not a non-feasible policy option.

Rationalizing the Private Sector: The Industry's Role

Despite its conservative approach to essential drugs policies, there is evidence that the drugs controversy has influenced the practices of pharmaceutical companies to an extent that some companies now appear to be genuinely aiming at more ethical promotion and a more rational distribution of drugs. An outstanding example is Ciba-Geigy, the company that was subject to a lot of criticism concerning its marketing practices in the 1970s. Ciba has established several measures to help manage potential or emerging product issues, including the Medical Product Committee, which monitors and constantly reassesses the safety of marketed products; the Product Information Policy and Product Communication Audit, which codify and control all drugs information; and the Product Issue Management and Early Warning Systems, which address drugs issues from a pharma-political perspective (Taylor and Miller, 1988). In 1985 the company introduced its own code of marketing practices, which is more stringent than the IFPMA code (SCRIP, 1988). The company appointed staff to audit adherence to the code.

At the end of 1986 the company began to develop an ambitious programme (Risk Assessment of Drugs: Analysis and Response) to help better understand the various factors involved in assessing drugs risks in today's complex society and to ensure that the company's methods of informing about and promoting its drugs did not contribute to that risk (Stearns, 1987). Ciba-Geigy is not the only company attempting to change its operations. Both the Searle company and a small US-based company, Alza, have been reviewing the type of information they are providing to prescribers and consumers (Chetley, 1990).

As a reaction to criticisms about their products, but also often for other (perhaps commercial) reasons, over the past decade many companies have withdrawn problem drugs from the market. It is, however, difficult to get an overview of these processes because withdrawals are often only announced to drugs regulatory authorities. Below, a number of examples of widely publicized 'voluntary' withdrawals are given as an illustration of this trend (HAI, 1991):

> In 1983 Ciba-Geigy announced that it would gradually withdraw its products containing clioquinol over a five year period, following an international campaign spearheaded by Olle Hanson and by the International Organization of Consumers Unions. The drugs had been associated with the severe neurological disorder called SMON (sub-acute myelo-optic neuropathy). As mentioned in Chapter 1, this drug caused paralysis and or partial loss of sight in over 10,000 people in Japan. This epidemic was the cause of much concern over the safety of drugs in the 1970s.

> In 1987 the German company, Hoechst, announced that it would withdraw all nomifensine products, in part due to the publicity generated by the German HAI partner, Buko. Nomifensine is an anti-depressant that had been associated with severe, in some cases fatal, blood disorders.

> In the same year a combination anti-diarrhoeal containing broxyquinoline and tetracycline was withdrawn by Sandoz following pressure from the HAI partner in Switzerland, the Berne Declaration Group; and Parke-Davis announce it would withdraw its streptomycin and chloramphenicol anti-diarrhoeal product in response to pressure from the Medical Lobby for Appropriate Marketing (MLAM).

> In 1989 Wellcome withdrew its kaolin/pectin anti-diarrhoeal, ADM, world-wide, following a UK television documentary.

In 1990 Janssen announced the withdrawal of its paediatric drops formulation of immodium (loperamide), following a UK television documentary which drew on the experience of HAI groups and health workers in Pakistan.

In these cases the voluntary withdrawal followed actions by consumer groups. There are numerous other cases in which governments forced the industrt to withdraw drugs from the market. In these cases usually whole categories of drugs are banned, thereby affecting a number of manufacturers. These are usually potentially hazardous drugs with no clear therapeutic value, or irrational combination drugs for which single preparations can be used as a cheaper and more appropriate alternative.

Pressure to ban and withdraw drugs has increased since the publication by the UN of the *Consolidated List of Products whose Consumption and/or Sale have been Banned, Withdrawn, Severely Restricted or not Approved by Governments* (UN, 1987). Many consumer organizations translated this UN list into handbooks, in which they list all the products available on the national markets that should be banned or severely restricted (HAIN, 1988; VHAI, 1986). Examples of government actions in this field are (*HAI News* 1985-1991):

In 1987 combination products containing dipyrone (an analgesic that can cause serious blood disorders) were banned in Pakistan, and another 605 drugs were deregistered as being harmful or ineffective.

Since 1979, when a drugs consultative committee began to review fixed dose combinations of drugs in India, 27 categories of drugs have been banned. One of these is the high dose estrogen/progestin combination products, which had been related to increased risk of birth defects if taken by pregnant women.

In 1985 Indonesia banned 90 irrational combination drugs. In 1986 nine hazardous drugs were banned in Malaysia and 220 irrational combination drugs in Peru. In 1991 Indonesia announced the banning of an additional 282 hazardous drugs and Yemen banned all drugs not listed on its essential drugs list.

The response of companies to these government bans have ranged from tacit acceptance to law suits, which delay the implementation of the order considerably. In some cases the banned drugs are still on the market because governments lack the capacity to monitor the implementation of orders.

Despite the voluntary and involuntary withdrawals of drugs from the market, there are still large numbers of irrational combination drugs, hazardous drugs and outdated drugs available in developing countries. A study by HAI (1988), for example, revealed that 60 per cent of the anti-diarrhoeals on the market in third world countries contained at least one antibiotic, which is an irrational and hazardous combination. Not only is it an irrational treatment for diarrhoea, but it also leads to a world-wide increase in resistance to antibiotics and consequent treatment failure when antibiotics could have been life saving. It is clear that in the coming decade pharmaceutical companies operating in countries where public pressure for rational drugs use is building up will be forced to rethink their product range in terms of safety, efficacy and medical need. A large number of developing countries will no longer allow potentially hazardous and irrational combination drugs on the market, leading to a world-wide decrease in the market for certain drugs. The response of companies to this situation will differ according to the extent to which they depend on such drugs for their returns and profits.

This leads us back to the question of applying the essential drugs concept to the private sector. In many countries the essential drugs concept has been adopted by government health programmes to help select and procure drugs for distribution to public health centres. However, more often than not these public health centres have to operate alongside private sector drugs distributors who sell branded drugs at higher prices. The thousands of drugs available in the private sector are often seen by consumers as attractive alternatives to the generics provided in the essential drugs programmes, especially if the health centres are continually having to face drugs shortages because of supply problems. Placing bans on hazardous and inessential categories of drugs can change this situation. However, a more radical approach involves confining *all* drugs imports and manufacturing to those that appear on the essential drugs list. Nigeria has recently adopted this restrictive policy. The extent to which the essential drugs concept can be effectively applied to both the public and private sector, however, largely depends on the power of the central government to control drugs manufacturing and distribution. With WHO's role diminished, governments are unlikely to receive much support for controlling the private sector from international agencies such as UNICEF and the World Bank. As we have seen, these agencies are disinclined to support such policies, for their focus is on strengthening basic health services for the poor in the public sector.

Another important trend is the expansion of the generic industry, particularly in the US. Generic drugs are unpatented drug products, including drugs whose patent has expired and those that have never been patented. The trend towards generic manufacturing has been most noticeable since the mid-1970s, when many of the world's best selling products began to lose their patents and governments were becoming increasingly cost conscious (WHO, 1988).

Among the developed countries, the US is the largest producer of generic drugs, with an estimated 35 per cent of the market in 1990. In that year only 21 of the top 100 prescription drugs in the US still had patent protection (Schaumann, 1985). In the US, the development of state substitution laws (giving pharmacists the right to supply generic drugs even when the prescription is for branded ones) has stimulated the demand for generics. In other countries the generics market is growing slowly. In 1988 the Philippines adopted the generics law, which demands industries to label their products with generic names and physicians to prescribe generic drugs. This law has led to much opposition from physicians defending their right to choose and from the industry. In most other developing countries the public sector supplies generic drugs and the private sector supplies branded drugs. Physicians and consumers tend to trust the branded products more than the generics. However, with more education about rational drugs, the generics market in these countries is also likely to increase.

It is interesting to note that the surge in generic manufacturing has created opportunities for governments of developing countries and NGOs to buy drugs at very favourable prices on the world market. Procurement is increasingly done by means of tendering or procuring through intermediary agencies, such as UNIPAC and the International Dispensary Association, which supply generic drugs at very favourable prices. This trend seems to have reduced the call for local production. In any case, it is increasingly being recognized that local production is a fairly expensive option for countries with small internal markets. The evaluation of DAP (LSHTM/KIT, 1989) revealed that seven of the 13 countries studied use essential drugs kits, mainly imported from Europe and usually from UNICEF's supply division, UNIPAC. Local production capacities were found to vary widely. The least developed countries produce small quantities of expensive and often non-essential drugs. Many of the countries with greater production capabilities were found to be hampered by not having the convertible currency with which to increase production to cost-effective levels.

In a comprehensive analysis of the pharmaceutical industry's role in public health and in the rational use of drugs, Chetley (1990) concludes that the industry will continue along its present path of confrontation versus cooperation. The extent to which one or the other will prevail, according to Chetley, 'will depend on the willingness of industry to ask itself some serious questions about its future directions'. Drugs safety, drugs prices and better training and information about drugs will be of ongoing concern to the actors in the field. In a world of limited resources, Chetley suggests that pressures will increase on companies continuing to develop 'me-too' drugs that do not offer a substantial therapeutic advantage over existing ones. With limited resources to train and inform prescribers and consumers on drugs, pressures to limit the number of drugs on the market will also continue. Chetley suggests that a middle way is possible, in which companies are offered better patent protection and profitable rewards for real innovation, for producing drugs that people really need and for acting in a responsible manner.

In Conclusion

The four interrelated trends discussed above leave us with a diffused DAP and a partially rationalized pharmaceutical environment. What seems to be needed, much as in the early 1980s, is a combination of technical support to countries implementing essential drugs programmes and advocacy to expand further the implementation of the essential drugs concept. The advocacy component, however, is likely to be less prominent in the 1990s.

In the above we have seen that national and international consumer, health and development organizations continue to call for the implementation of comprehensive essential drugs policies. It is clear that in the coming decade pharmaceutical companies operating in countries where there is mounting public pressure for rational drugs use will need to rethink their product range in terms of safety, efficacy, cost and medical need. A large number of developing countries will no longer tolerate irrational combinations of potentially hazardous drugs and this will considerably reduce the market for them. The generics industry will further reduce the market for unnecessarily expensive drugs. The response of companies to this situation will differ according to the extent to which they depend on hazardous drugs, irrational combinations and expensive 'me-too' products for their returns and profits.

Yet, various national industrial associations, government representatives, politicians and influential medical professional bodies operating within the drugs-exporting countries often seem to succeed in limiting the effectiveness of the programmes. Also, public action to control the private sector may be less effective than in the 1970s and 1980s in that the international political environment (since the fall of Eastern Europe's communist regimes and the changes in the Soviet Union) is unsympathetic towards any form of state control over private enterprise. There are, of course, exceptions. Sudan and Nigeria have recently adopted regulations that restrict the number of drugs in the private sector to those on the essential drugs list. But it remains to be seen whether or not these policies really will create a rationalized market. Nigeria, for one, is confronted with immense problems, including the smuggling of drugs into the country and the production of fake drugs (Pole, 1989).

In the past WHO could make a difference by giving authoritative support to progressive initiatives. Under the present leadership, however, it is questionable whether it would be willing to take on such an advocacy role. It is more likely to confine itself to giving technical support when needed. Neither are the other international actors, UNICEF and the World Bank, likely to support policies that would affect private sector interests.

We have argued that the drugs themes in the 1990s are likely to be financing, rational use and choice. The focus will be on implementing essential drugs programmes and not on more political policy issues, such as the universal coverage of the essential drugs concept, or the application of the essential drugs concept to the private sector.

By paying more attention to community participation, the Bamako Initiative is likely to help integrate PHC and essential drugs programmes in sub-Saharan Africa. We also argued that the emphasis in international health on the accessibility and rational use of contraceptives and on the need to distribute condoms more effectively in the light of the AIDS epidemic, call for further integration of essential drugs and family planning programmes.

Though theoretically desirable, this integration is, however, unlikely to occur in practice. Given the scope of the Bamako Initiative, community participation tends to be confined to those who pay for their drugs or, in some cases, manage the revenue. UNICEF has yet to utilize its potential to integrate training on the rational use of drugs into its health education programmes. The vertical nature of family planning programmes and the prevailing focus on population rather than health also limit the feasibility of an integrated approach.

In the light of the world economic recession, the exploding world population and the AIDS epidemic, WHO could play a crucial role by helping to redesign the frameworks of PHC, essential drugs and family planning. However, the emphasis at present seems to be on technical support, not policy or advocacy. With WHO's international advocacy role diminishing, much will depend on the political will of governments to implement comprehensive national drugs policies. The growing critical mass in developing countries calling for such policies is perhaps the most important trend in this regard. One can but hope that the advocacy efforts of the 1980s have reached such a wide audience and given so much credibility to the essential drugs concept that the essential drugs movement can no longer be stopped.

References

Bruce, J. (1989) *Fundamental elements of the quality of care: A simple framework*. The Population Council, Programs Division, Working Papers No 1. New York: Population Council

Chabot, H.T.J. (1988) 'The Bamako Initiative', letter in *The Lancet*, 1 December

Chela, C.M., I.D. Campbell and Z. Siankanga (1989) 'Clinical care as part of integrated AIDS management in a Zambian rural community'. Unpublished ms

Chetley, A. (1990) *A healthy business: World health and the pharmaceutical industry*. London: Zed Books

DAP/WHO (1990) *Progress report 1990*. Geneva: DAP/WHO

DAP/WHO (1991) 'African initiative'. Internal paper presented to the Management Advisory Committee, February

Essential Drugs Monitor (1991) 'MAC approves US$24 million DAP budget'. *Essential Drugs Monitor*, 11 (20)

Foster, S. (1991) 'Supply and use of essential drugs in sub-Saharan Africa: Some issues and possible solutions'. *Social Science and Medicine*, 32 (11): 1201-19

HAI (1988) *The wrong drugs for diarrhoea*. Amsterdam: HAI

HAI (1991) *Ten years campaigning for rational drug use*. Amsterdam: HAI

HAI News (1985-1991)

HAIN (1988) *Drug handbook: Banned, withdrawn and restricted drugs in the Philippines*. Quezon City: HAIN

Hancock, G. (1989) *The lords of poverty*. New York: Atlantic Monthly Press

Hardon, A. (ed.) (1990) *Women and pharmaceuticals bulletin*. Amsterdam: WEMOS/HAI

Hardon, A.P. (1991) *Confronting ill health: Self-care medicines and the poor in Manila*. Quezon City: HAIN

Hodgkin, C. (1991) Personal communication, March

Kanji, N. (1989) 'Charging for drugs in Africa: UNICEF's Bamako Initiative'. *Health Policy and Planning*, 4 (2): 110-20

Kanji, N. and F. Manji (1991) 'From development to sustained crisis: Structural adjustment, equity and health'. *Social Science and Medicine*, 33 (9): 985-93

Katabira, E. and R. Goodgame (1989) *AIDS care: Diagnostic and treatment strategies for health workers*. Entebbe: MOH

LSHTM/KIT (1989) *Evaluation of WHO's Action Programme on Essential Drugs*. London: LSHTM/KIT

Lopez, R. and A. Kroeger (eds) (1990) *Mobilidad y medicamentos en Peru y Bolivia. Un estudio sobre mobilidad, use de servicios de salud y consumo de medicamentos con una intervencion educativa*. Lima: Grafico Bellido

Over, M., S. Bertozzi, J. Chin, B. N'Galy and K. Nyamuryekung'e (1988) 'The direct and indirect costs of HIV infection in developing countries: The cases of Zaire and Tanzania'. In A. Fleming et al. (eds) *The global impact of AIDS*, New York: Alan R. Liss

Pole, D. (1989) *Drug distribution and fake drugs in Nigeria: Proceedings of a workshop*. Lagos: IMI

Remstrad, L.G. (1987) *Nigeria essential drugs project, information, education and communication, report of a WHO mission*. Geneva: DAP/WHO

Schaumann, L. et al. (1985) *A generics milestone*, vol 1. Menlo Park: SRI International

SCRIP (1988) *Ciba-Geigy reaffirms open policy*. SCRIP 1377

SCRIP (1988a) *All changes at the WHO*, quoting *The Lancet*, 28 May, 1201-2

Stearns, B. (1987) 'RAD-AR: Homing in on risk'. *Ciba-Geigy Journal*, 2

Taylor, D. and D. Miller (1988) *RAD-AR: An executive summary*. Basle: Ciba-Geigy

UN (1987) *Consolidated list of products whose consumption and/or sale have been banned, withdrawn, severely restricted or not approved by governments*. New York: UN

UNDP (1991) *Human development report*. London: Oxford University Press

UNFPA (1991) *World population report*. New York: UNFPA

UNICEF (1988) *The Bamako Initiative*. Panel 188 in UNICEF's The State of the World's Children. London: Oxford University Press

UNICEF (1990) *Revitalizing primary health care/maternal and child health: The Bamako Initiative*. E/ICEF/1990/L.3. New York: UNICEF

UNICEF (1991) *The Bamako Initiative: Progress report.* E/ICEF/1991, New York: UNICEF

UNICEF/HAI/OXFAM (1990) *Report on the International Study Conference on Community Financing in Primary Health Care.* Freetown 23-30 September 1989, Amsterdam: HAI/UNICEF

VHAI (1986) *Dangerous medicines: The fact, banned and bannable drugs.* New Delhi: VHAI, 1986.

WHO (1988) *The world drug situation.* Geneva: WHO

Williams, D. (1987) *The specialized agencies and the United Nations.* London: C. Hurst

World Bank (1991) *World development report: Poverty.* Washington: World Bank

Appendix

WHO Ethical Criteria and IFPMA Code of Pharmaceutical Marketing Practices — Review and Comment

WHO: On Promotion

Active promotion within a country should take place only with respect to drugs legally available in the country. Promotion should be in keeping with national health policies and in compliance with national regulations, as well as with voluntary standards where they exist. All promotion making claims concerning medicinal drugs should be reliable, accurate, truthful, informative, balanced, up to date, capable of substantiation and in good taste. It should not contain misleading or unverifiable statements or omissions likely to induce medically unjustifiable drugs use or to give rise to undue risks. The word 'safe' should only be used if properly qualified. Comparison of products should be factual, fair and capable of substantiation. Promotional material should not be designed so as to disguise its real nature.

IFPMA: On Promotion (Obligations)

The industry in general obligations, undertook 'to ensure that all products it makes available for prescription purposes to the public are backed by the fullest technological service and have full regard to the needs of public health; to produce pharmaceutical products under adequate procedures and strict quality assurance; to base the claims for substances and formulations on valid scientific evidence, thus determining the therapeutic indications and conditions of use; to provide scientific information with objectivity and good taste, with scrupulous regard for truth, and with clear statements with respect to indications, contraindications, tolerance and toxicity; to use complete candour in dealings with public health officials, health care professionals and the public.'

HAI Comments: On Promotion

(1) The promotion of prescription only products should not be permitted directly or indirectly to the general public. (2) The usefulness of the promotion of OTC products to the general public is in some doubt, as many of these products are for trivial or self-limiting conditions and are often of doubtful efficacy. Their promotion encourages a 'pill for every ill' mentality which detracts from preventive health care, wastes resources and can expose consumers to unnecessary risks. Thus, promotion of OTC products to the general public should not be permitted. (3) Promotion to health workers must be consistent with existing national health and drugs policies, taking into accouant recommended treatment regimes, where these are in effect. (4) The volume of promotion for a particular product must be consistent with that product's utility in treating the major disease conditions prevalent in a particular country. Promotion of products for self-limiting or trivial conditions should not be permitted. (5) As no drug is completely without risk, the word 'safe', with or without qualification, should not be permitted in any promotional material. (6) All promotion for pharmaceutical products must be accurate, factual, balanced and up to date. It must conform to legal requirements and to standards of good taste, and be provided in a language readily understandable to the person who will use it. It must not mislead, either directly or by implication, by omission or information, or by unverifiable statements.

WHO: On Advertisements to the General Public

Advertisements to the general public should help people to make rational decisions on the use of drugs determined to be legally available without a prescription. While they should take account of people's legitimate desire for information regarding their health they should not take undue advantage of people's concern for their health. They should not generally be permitted for prescription drugs or to promote drugs for certain serious conditions that can be treated only by qualified health practitioners, for which certain countries have established lists. While health education aimed at children is highly desirable, drug advertisements should not be directed at children. Advertisements may claim that a drug can cure, prevent, or relieve an ailment only if this can be substantiated. They should also indicate, where applicable, appropriate limitations to the use of the drug.

IFPMA: On Advertisements to the General Public

Not covered by the IFPMA Code. The World Federation of Proprietary Medicine Manufacturers (WFPMM) has, however, developed guidelines for the production of voluntary codes of advertising practice.

HAI Comments: On Advertisements to the General Public

(1) As mentioned above, advertisements to the general public for non-prescription drugs should not be permitted. There is a clear acceptance by the industry that advertising aimed at children is certainly not ethical or advisable. A recent study by the Association of British Pharmaceutical Industries found 'the average British patient has a reading age of nine'. Thus, it is difficult to justify promotion of any drugs to the public. (2) If public advertising is permitted, advertisements must not be directed at children. (3) If public advertising is permitted, all advertisements must carry a clear and prominent statement advising users of the products to read and follow the instructions for use on the package, label or package insert of the product, and if they are unsure of what any of the directions mean, to consult a physician or pharmacist before taking the product. (4) If public advertising is permitted, advertisements for products that should be avoided during pregnancy and lactation should contain graphic warning symbols.

WHO: On Samples

Free samples of legally available prescription drugs may be provided in modest quantities to prescribers, generally on request. Countries vary in their practices regarding the provision of free samples of non-prescription drugs to the general public, some countries permitting it, some not. Also, a distinction has to be made between provision of free drugs by health agencies for the care of certain groups and the provision of free samples to the general public for promotional purposes. The provision of free samples of non-prescription drugs to the general public for promotional purposes is difficult to justify from a health perspective. If this practice is legally permitted in any country, it should be handled with great restraint.

IFPMA: On Samples

Samples may be supplied to the medical and allied professions to familiarize them with the products, to enable them to gain experience with the product in their practice, or upon request. The IFPMA Code does not deal explicitly with samples to the general public. The WFPMM Guidelines do not mention sampling to the public.

HAI Comments: On Samples

(1) The routine provision of samples of prescription or non-prescription drugs to health workers, health institutions, or the general public should not be permitted. (2) Supplies of prescription drugs, in sufficient quantity for controlled and approved clinical trials, or other legitimate research, may be permitted.

WHO: On Symposia and other Scientific Meetings

Symposia are useful for disseminating information. The objective scientific content of such meetings should be paramount and presentations by independent scientists and health professionals are helpful to this end. Their educational value may be enhanced if they are organized by scientific or professional bodies. The fact of sponsorship by a pharmaceutical manufacturer or distributor should be clearly stated in advance, at the meeting and in any proceedings. The latter should accurately reflect the presentations and discussions. Entertainment or other hospitality and any gifts offered to members of the medical and allied professions should be secondary to the main purpose of the meeting and should be kept to a modest level.

IFPMA: On Symposia and other Scientific Meetings

Symposia, congresses and the like are indispensable for the dissemination of knowledge and experience. Scientific objectives should be the principal focus in arranging such meetings, and entertainment and other hospitality shall not be inconsistent with such objectives.

HAI Comments: On Symposia and other Scientific Meetings

(1) The organization by pharmaceutical manufacturers or distributors of symposia and other scientific meetings should only be permitted if approval for such a meeting has been granted by the relevant national or international health worker association, health institution or government department; an independent panel of scientists and/or health workers has been set up to review the content of the meeting; and full disclosure of the sponsorship is stated in all communications related to the meeting, and at the meeting itself. (2) Partial sponsorship of such meetings may be permitted if such sponsorship is requested by the organizers, subject to the full disclosure of the sponsorship.

Index

ACDIMA (Arab Company for Drug
  Industries and Medical
  Appliances), 15
Addis Ababa, 100
Advertising Standards Authority, 6
Africa/African, 13, 25, 28, 32, 40, 41,
  111, 114, 117
AFRO (Africa Regional Office), 25,
  36, 38, 40, 41, 42, 79, 111
Agarwal, A., 9
AIDS (Auto-immune Deficiency
  Syndrome), 7, 110, 113, 117-18,
  124, 125
ALIFABOL, 82, 83
Alma Ata, 13
Alza, 120
Andean region, 15, 39
Andhra Pradesh, 100
Angola, 99
Antezana, Dr, 42, 44, 111
APEC (Action Programme for
  Economic Cooperation), 12
Aquino, President, 72
Argentina, 3, 4, 19
Armstrong, 33, 35
Asia/Asian, 6, 14, 25, 32, 39, 72
Asian Development Bank, 94, 95
ASOFAR, 82
Association of British Pharmaceutical
  Industry, 72, 129
Balasubramanium, K., 15
Bamako Initiative, 40, 41, 42, 79,
  111, 114, 115, 118, 124, 125
Bamako, Mali, 79
Bangladesh, 2, 3, 36, 53, 71-2, 73,
  75, 79, 84, 88, 92, 95, 98, 99, 101,
  104
Bannenberg, W., x, 73, 87

Basch, P.F., 2
Batia, J.C., 102
Beechams, 88
Benin, 114
Berne, 50, 120
Berthoud, S., 73
Bibile, S., 9, 10
Bledsoe, C.H., 102
Bolivia, 15, 39, 82, 83
Boots, 88
Brazil, 3, 4, 9, 19, 100, 101
breast milk substitutes, 25, 31, 43, 49,
  54, 59
Britain/British, 4, 5, 6, 71, 72, 77, 85,
  88, 105, 107, 130
British Medical Association, 105
British Pharmaceutical Industries,
  129
Brooks, R. A., 57
Bruce, J., 119
Budapest, 15,
Buko, 120
Burghart, R., 102
Burundi, 52, 70, 72, 73, 92, 115
Cameroon, 112
Capo, L.R., 8
Caribbean, 15, 117
Central de Medicamentos, 9
Chabot, H.T.J., 114
Chela, C.M., 118
Chetley, A., 31, 37, 38, 50, 54, 57,
  97, 106, 111, 120, 123
Chile, 15, 51
China, 71
chloramphenicol, 6, 8, 100, 120
Chowdhury, S., 75
Chowdhury, Z., 75
Christian Medical Association, 116

Christian Medical Commission, 105
Ciba-Geigy, 5, 72, 119, 120
Cliff, J., 82
clioquinol, 5, 120
Cohen, Dr, 107
Collier, J., 5, 6
Colombia, 15, 39, 71, 73, 74, 92, 93
Colombo, 12, 39
Commonwealth Pharmaceutical
   Association, 105
Copenhagen, 15, 41, 77, 95, 96
COPPTECS (Cooperative
   Pharmaceutical Production and
   Technology Centres), 15
Costa Rica/Costa Rican, 8, 9, 10
Cuba, 4, 8, 9, 14, 51
Dag Hammarskjöld Foundation, 54
DANIDA (Danish International
   Development Agency), 33, 35, 44,
   77, 78, 79, 86
Democratic Yemen, 70, 75, 79, 84,
   94, 97, 99, 105
Denmark/Danish, x, 30, 33, 77, 78,
   96, 107
DIAC (Drug Information and Action
   Centre), 116
dipyrone, 100
DMP (Division of Drug Management
   and Policies), 44
DPM (Drug Policies and
   Management) division, 27, 28, 29,
   31, 42, 43, 45, 65, 111
Dukes, M.N.G., 3
Dunlop Committee, 5
Dunne, Dr John, 44
Dutch, see Netherlands
Eastern Europe, ix, 11, 124
Ecuador, 15, 39, 100
Egypt, 3, 4, 8, 9, 10, 19
El Salvador, 8
EMRO (Eastern Mediterranean
   Regional Office), 25, 36, 38, 39, 74
Ethiopia, 100
EURO (European Regional Office),
   25
extradiol, 4
Fabricant, S.J., 54
Fajnzylber, F., 4
Fassin, D., 101
Fattorusso, Dr., 42
Foster, J., 14

Foster, S., 117
France/French, 4, 32, 36, 77, 106,
   107
Frelimo, 9
Frères des Hommes, 105
Galal, E.E., 8, 9
Gambia, The, 52, 72
Geneva, 25, 27, 29, 30, 31, 34, 35,
   36, 39, 42, 50, 78, 105, 111
George, S., 5
Georgetown, Guyana, 12
Germany/German, 3, 4, 11, 71, 72,
   76, 82, 88, 94, 106, 107, 120
Ghana, 51, 100, 101, 112
Gilbert, D., 5
Glaxo, 88
Gonashasthaya Kendra, 75
Goodgame, R., 117
Goubaud, M., 102
Grant, James, 40, 41
Greenhalgh, T., 84, 100
Guatemala, 8
Guest, I., 53
Guinea, 12, 115
Haak, H., 101
HAI (Health Action International),
   31, 37, 48, 49, 50, 51, 53, 54, 58,
   59, 61, 62, 105, 114, 116, 120, 121,
   128, 129, 130, 131
HAIN (Health Action Information
   Network), 116, 121
Hancock, G., 112
Hansen, J., 73
Hanson, Olle, 120
Hardon, A.P., 100, 102, 116, 118
Hathi Committee, 84
Havana, 16, 17
Heller, T., 12
Helling-Borda, M., 16, 26
Heritage Foundation, 57, 59, 60
Herxheimer, A., 6
Hirschorn, N., 54
Hodgkin, C., 111
Hoechst, 10, 11, 120
Hoffman-La Roche, 19, 70, 72
Hogerzeil, H., 99
Holland, see Netherlands
Hushang, A., 25
IBFAN (International Baby Food
   Action Network), 31, 49, 50
ICI, 88

ICIFI (International Council of Infant Food Industries), 31, 50
IFPMA (International Federation of Pharmaceutical Manufacturers' Associations), 19, 29, 30, 31, 32, 39, 48, 49, 50, 51, 52, 53, 55, 56, 58, 59, 61, 62, 120, 128-31
ILO (International Labour Office), 13, 25, 29
India/Indian, 4, 5, 7, 8, 11, 12, 19, 25, 71, 84, 100, 102, 121
Indian Institute of Public Administration, 5
Indonesia, 28, 39, 71, 74, 86, 92, 93, 99, 101, 121
INFACT (Infant Formula Action Coalition), 50
INRUD (International Network for the Rational Use of Drugs), 116
Institute of British Advertisers, 6
International Dispensary Association, 123
International Federation of Pharmacists, 105
Interpharma, 72, 73
IOCU (International Organization of Consumers Unions), 53, 60
IOMS (International Organization Monitoring Services), 54, 55, 57, 58, 59, 60
Isenalumhe, A., 101
Islam, N., 94, 95
Janssen, 121
Japan/Japanese, 5, 44, 76, 94, 106, 107, 110, 120
JCHP (Joint Committee on Health Policy), 15, 40, 42
Jelliffe, D., 49
Kanji, N.G., 75, 76, 77, 79, 82, 94, 95, 96, 99, 113, 114
Katabira, E., 117
Kay, D.A., 6
Kenya/Kenyan, 12, 33, 36, 37, 40, 52, 70, 72, 85-6, 92, 93, 97, 98, 104
Korn, J., 12
Krishnaswamy, K., 100
Kroeger, A., 116
Lall, S., 10, 11, 14
Latin American, 14, 113
Lauridsen, Dr. E., 3, 33, 42, 61
Le Grande, A., 100

Leonard, S., 55
Lerman, S., 101
Librium, 19
Lomotil, 31, 51
loperamide, 121
Lopez, R., 116
Lunde, P.K.M., 3, 6, 13, 14, 94
Madagascar, 112
Mahler, Dr Halfden, 1, 6, 13, 14, 20, 25, 29, 41, 42, 43, 44, 57, 58, 104, 106, 107, 110
Malawi, 115
Malaysia, 39, 121
Maldives, 72
Marshall, R., 88
Marshall Plan, 72
Martinussen, J., 36
Marzagao, M., 10
Masland, T., 88
Medawar, Charles, 4, 6, 9, 19, 54
Médecins sans Frontières, 105
MEDIMOC, 9, 76, 81, 82
Mediterranean, 25, 75
Melrose, D., 3, 7, 51
Mende, 102
Mexico, 4, 6, 8, 19, 42
Miller, D., 120
Mingst, K., 29
Mozambique, 8, 9, 10, 14, 70, 76, 79, 80-2, 88, 92, 97, 98, 99, 103, 104
Mujib, Sheik, 71
Muller, M., 3, 10, 11, 15
Nairobi, 37, 52, 53, 54, 55, 57, 58, 60, 61, 63, 107, 115
Nakajima, Dr Hiroshi, 27, 42, 43, 51, 110, 111
Nasser, Gamal Abdel, 8
Nestlé, 49, 50
Netherlands, The, 30, 51, 52, 53, 62, 77, 82, 107
New York, 42, 54, 78, 96
Nichter, M., 102
Nigeria/Nigerian, 70, 88, 92, 101, 112, 115, 122, 124
Nomifensine, 121
Norway/Nordic countries, 13, 30, 37, 51, 53, 57, 58, 62
ORT (oral rehydration treatment), 99, 101, 111
Over, M., 118

Overseas Development Agency, 97, 105
Oviawe, O., 101
OXFAM, 51, 105, 114
PAHO (Pan-American Health Organization), 25, 39
Pakistan, 8, 9, 121
Papua New Guinea, 14
Parke-Davis, 120
Patel, S.J., 16
PDRY (People's Democratic Republic of Yemen), 75, 92
PEDLIZ (Proposed Essential Drugs List of Zimbabwe), 87
Pemba Island, Tanzania, 72
penicillin, 18, 102
Peretz, Mr Michael, 29, 52, 53
Peretz, S.M., 30
Peru, 8, 14, 15, 39, 121
Pfizer, 10, 72
PHA (Pharmaceuticals unit within WHO), 26, 27, 33, 35, 38, 42, 44, 111
PHC (primary health care), 25, 42, 45, 68, 77, 78, 79, 83, 86, 87, 94, 95, 97, 100, 111, 113, 114, 116, 117, 119, 124, 125
Philippines, The, 39, 42, 71, 72, 74, 100, 101, 102, 116, 122
Piachaud, D., 11
PMA (Pharmaceutical Manufacturers Association), 10, 29, 30, 58, 72
Pole, D., 124
Portugal/Portuguese, 81
Price, L., 100
progesterone, 4
Prudencio, I., 82, 83
Reagan, Ronald, 48, 72
Reich, M., 48
Remstrad, L.G., 115
Rhodesia, see Zimbabwe
Rifkin, S., x, 13, 36
Roche, see Hoffman-La Roche
Rolt, F., 72, 84
Sandoz, 72, 120
Scandinavia, 45, 94
Schaumann, L., 122
Schrijver, N., 29
Searle, G.D., 31, 120
SEARO (South-East Asia Regional Office), 25, 39

Segall, M., 10
Sekhar, C., 100, 102
Senegal, 100
Shiva, M., 84
SIDA (Swedish International Development Agency), 86, 95
Sierra Leone, 102
Sikkink, K., 25
Silverman, M., 6, 7
Singapore, 39
SMON (sub-acute myelo-optic neuropathy), 120
Somalia, 52
South Africa/n, ix, 81, 87
South American, 4
Soviet Union, 71, 124
SPC (State Pharmaceutical Corporation), 10, 11
Sri Lanka/Sri Lankan, 8, 9, 10, 11, 14, 101
Sri Ngernyuang, L., 100
Stearns, B., 120
Stenzl, C., 12, 15
Sterky, G., 101
Streefland, Peter, x
streptomycin, 8, 120
sub-Saharan Africa, 112, 113, 114, 115, 124
Sudan, 51, 92, 97, 98, 99, 124
sulphonamide/s, 8, 18
Sweden/Swedish, 26, 54, 77, 82
Swedish Board of Health, 26
Swiss Development Agency, 73
Switzerland/Swiss, 3, 4, 6, 49, 50, 51, 52, 72, 76, 88, 106, 107, 120
Syntex, 4
Tan, M., 72
Tanzania, 3, 12, 33, 36, 37, 40, 41, 52, 72, 77-8, 79, 84, 92, 94, 96, 97, 98, 118
Taylor, D., 120
TCDC (Technical Cooperation among the Developing Countries), 28
Teeling-Smith, G., 7
tetracycline, 8, 10, 101, 120
Thailand, 2, 39, 74, 100, 101, 116
thalidomide, 5, 12, 26
Tiefenbacher, M.P., 11
Tognoni, G., 82, 83
Togo, 112

Tomson, G., 101
Uganda, 117
UN High Commission on Refugees,
   105
UNCTAD (United Nations
   Conference on Trade and
   Technology), 4, 9, 10, 12, 14, 15,
   16, 17, 24, 27, 51
UNCTC (United Nations Centre on
   Transnational Corporations), 4, 9,
   10, 18, 19
UNDP (United Nations Development
   Programme), 16, 17, 95, 112, 113
UNESC (United Nations Economic
   and Social Council), 2, 4, 8, 9, 10,
   19
UNESCO (United Nations
   Educational, Cultural and Scientific
   Organization), 29, 59
UNFPA (United Nations Family
   Planning Association), 119
UNICEF (United Nations Children's
   Fund), 12, 14, 15, 33, 36, 37, 39,
   40, 41, 42, 50, 56, 69, 76, 77-8, 79,
   82, 95, 96, 111, 112, 113, 114, 115,
   122, 123, 124, 125
UNIDO (United Nations Industrial
   Development Organization), 4, 12,
   14, 15, 16, 17, 24, 27
UNIPAC, 37, 41, 75, 76, 77, 79, 82,
   86, 95, 96, 123
United Kingdom, 3
Uppsala, 26
US (United States), 4, 29, 30, 31, 43,
   44, 59, 71, 72, 74, 76, 85, 94, 106,
   107, 110, 113, 120, 122
USAID (United States Agency for
   International Development), 82, 95
Valium, 19, 70
Venezuela, 15, 39
Vietnam, 92, 98, 99
Walker, G., 3, 4, 9, 14, 15
War on Want, 49, 69
Wellcome, 88, 120
Wells, C., 29
Williams, D., 112
Wolffers, I., 102
Wondergem, P., 101
World Bank, 1, 40, 94, 95, 112, 113,
   114, 122, 124

WPRO (Western Pacific Regional
   Office), 25, 36, 39, 42, 61
YAR (Yemen Arab Republic), 70,
   75, 84, 97
Yemen, 84, 92, 101, 121, see also
   PDRY and YAR
Yudkin, J.S., 3
ZEDAP (Zimbabwean Essential
   Drugs Programme, 87
Zimbabwe, 70, 87-8, 92, 94

Zed Books Ltd

is a publisher whose international and Third World lists span:

- **Women's Studies**
- **Development**
- **Environment**
- **Current Affairs**
- **International Relations**
- **Children's Studies**
- **Labour Studies**
- **Cultural Studies**
- **Human Rights**
- **Indigenous Peoples**
- **Health**

We also specialize in Area Studies where we have extensive lists in African Studies, Asian Studies, Caribbean and Latin American Studies, Middle East Studies, and Pacific Studies.

For further information about books available from Zed Books, please write to: Catalogue Enquiries, Zed Books Ltd, 57 Caledonian Road, London N1 9BU. Our books are available from distributors in many countries (for full details, see our catalogues), including:

In the USA
Humanities Press International, Inc., 165 First Avenue,
Atlantic Highlands, New Jersey 07716.
Tel: (908) 872 1441;
Fax: (908) 872 0717.

In Canada
DEC, 229 College Street, Toronto, Ontario M5T 1R4.
Tel: (416) 971 7051.

In Australia
Wild and Woolley Ltd, 16 Darghan Street, Glebe, NSW 2037.

In India
Bibliomania, C-236 Defence Colony, New Delhi 110 024.

In Southern Africa
David Philip Publisher (Pty) Ltd, PO Box 408, Claremont 7735,
South Africa.